'The axe had never sounded'

place, people and heritage of
Recherche Bay, Tasmania

'The axe had never sounded'

place, people and heritage of Recherche Bay, Tasmania

John Mulvaney

E PRESS

Published by ANU E Press and Aboriginal History Incorporated
Aboriginal History Monograph 14

National Library of Australia
Cataloguing-in-Publication entry

Mulvaney, D. J. (Derek John), 1925- .
The axe had never sounded : place, people and heritage of
Recherche Bay, Tasmania.

Bibliography.
ISBN 9781921313202 (pbk.)
ISBN 9781921313219 (online)

1. Aboriginal Tasmanians - Tasmania - Recherche Bay. 2.
Cultural property - Political aspects - Tasmania -
Recherche Bay. 3. Recherche Bay (Tas.) - Discovery and
exploration - French. 4. Recherche Bay (Tas.) - History.
I. Title.

994.62

Aboriginal History is administered by an Editorial Board which is responsible for all unsigned material. Views and opinions expressed by the author are not necessarily shared by Board members.

The Committee of Management and the Editorial Board
Peter Read (Chair), Rob Paton (Treasurer/Public Officer), Ingereth Macfarlane (Secretary/ Managing Editor), Richard Baker, Gordon Briscoe, Ann Curthoys, Brian Egloff, Geoff Gray, Niel Gunson, Christine Hansen, Luise Hercus, David Johnston, Steven Kinnane, Harold Koch, Isabel McBryde, Ann McGrath, Frances Peters-Little, Kaye Price, Deborah Bird Rose, Peter Radoll, Tiffany Shellam

Editors Ingereth Macfarlane and Kaye Price
Copy editor Geoff Hunt

Contacting Aboriginal History
All correspondence should be addressed to Aboriginal History,
Box 2837 GPO Canberra, 2601, Australia.
Sales and orders for journals and monographs, and journal subscriptions:
T Boekel, email: sales@aboriginalhistory.org, tel or fax: +61 2 6230 7054
www.aboriginalhistory.org

ANU E Press
All correspondence should be addressed to:
ANU E Press, The Australian National University, Canberra ACT 0200, Australia
Email: anuepress@anu.edu.au, http://epress.anu.edu.au

Aboriginal History Inc. is a part of the Australian Centre for Indigenous History, Research School of Social Sciences, The Australian National University and gratefully acknowledges the support of the History Program, RSSS and the National Centre for Indigenous Studies, The Australian National University.

Cover design by Teresa Prowse

Apart for any fair dealing for the purpose of private study, research, criticism or review, as permitted under the Copyright Act, no part of this publication may be reproduced by any process whatsoever without the written permission of the publisher.

This edition © 2007 ANU E Press and Aboriginal History Inc

'We were filled with admiration at the sight of these ancient forests, in which the axe had never sounded'
        Labillardière 1792

Contents

Foreword	xi
Introduction	xvii
Acknowledgements	xxi
Chapter 1. Setting Out	1
The Officers	3
The Savants	5
Ships and Stores	10
Chapter 2. Recherche Bay	13
Recherche Bay, revisited summer 1793	19
Chapter 3. Naturalists Ashore	25
Chapter 4. Botanising	31
The Garden	36
Chapter 5. Measuring and Charting	41
Chapter 6. Seeking the Tasmanians	53
Chapter 7. Meeting the Tasmanians	63
Chapter 8. An Archaeological Heritage	75
Chapter 9. Labillardière's Luck	81
Chapter 10. Retrospect: Recherche Bay, History and Anthropology	87
Chapter 11. The Chaotic Years	93
Whaling	93
Piracy on the Brig Cyprus	96
Chapter 12. Lady Jane at Recherche Bay	103
Chapter 13. Good and Bad Times	107
Coal Mining	110
James Craig	113
Chapter 14. The Concept of Heritage	117
Chapter 15. National Heritage Nomination	127
The Dénouement	134
References	137

Illustrations

Aerial view of northern area of Recherche Bay, 2005. Senator Bob Brown	xi
Recherche Bay, north-eastern peninsula from the air, 2005. Senator Bob Brown	xiii
Map 1 South-eastern Tasmania	xiv
Map 2 Recherche Bay, showing places mentioned in the text	xv
Recherche and *Espérance* under way. Watercolour by Frédéric Roux, Musée National de la Marine, Paris	1
Antoine-Joseph-Bruny d'Entrecasteaux, 1737-1793. National Library of Australia	2
Jacques-Julien Houton de Labillardière. National Library of Australia	6
Recherche Bay entrance from Bennetts Point, 2003. John Mulvaney	14
Looking towards Mt La Perouse from the 1792 beach, 2003. John Mulvaney	16
The enigmatic stone structure at Bennetts Point, 2003. John Mulvaney	18
Beautemps-Beaupré's chart showing the 1792 harbour anchorage. National Library of Australia	21
Type specimen of *Eucalyptus globulus* (blue gum). National Library of Australia	33
The 'garden' in 2003, outlined by rocks. John Mulvaney	38
The dip needle used by Rossel. D'Entrecasteaux journal, 1808	42
de Borda's 'cercle répétiteur' (left) and 'cercle de reflexion' (right). Musée National de la Marine, Paris	43
Beautemps-Beaupré's chart of Rocky Bay, southern Recherche Bay. National Library of Australia	46
Beautemps-Beaupré's chart of D'Entrecasteaux Channel. National Library of Australia	49
View of Rocky Bay from 1793 watering place, 2006. John Mulvaney	50
'Aborigines of Van Diemen's Land preparing a meal', ['Sauvages du Cap de Diemen preparant leur repas'], Jean Piron, 1793. National Library of Australia	66
'Tasmanians preparing a meal from the sea', ['Peche des sauvages du Cap de Diemen'], Jean Piron, 1793. National Library of Australia	68
Quiet Cove, 2006. John Mulvaney	69

Imlay shore-based whaling station, 2006. John Mulvaney	94
Fisher Point pilot station and pub, 2006. John Mulvaney	95
Woodcut of *Cyprus* castaways attributed to W. B. Gould, 1829. Archives Office of Tasmania	97
Machinery at Leprena mill site, 2006. John Mulvaney	108
Leprena timber mill site, 2006. John Mulvaney	109
Timber mill remains, Cockle Creek, 2006. John Mulvaney	110
Base of coal storage bin, Evoralls Point, 2006. John Mulvaney	111
Overturned tram engine near Evoralls Point, 2006. John Mulvaney	112
James Craig (then the *Clan Macleod*), New York harbour 1890. Sydney Heritage Fleet	113
James Craig submerged, 1960s, Recherche Bay. Sydney Heritage Fleet	114
The logging track through Southport Lagoon Conservation Area, 2005. Senator Bob Brown	123
Mulvaney addressing the April 2005 rally. Tom Baxter	129

Tables

Table 1 Rossel's magnetic intensity measurements	45

Foreword

Aerial view of northern area of Recherche Bay, 2005. Senator Bob Brown

Northern Recherche Bay from the air. D'Entrecasteaux River at bottom; Leprena mill site near beach at right. In 1792 ships anchored in the last embayment before the harbour entrance. Photograph by Senator Bob Brown, 2005

Recherche Bay, at the southern tip of Tasmania, combines exquisite natural beauty with a rich, exciting human history.

In 1792, French Vice-Admiral Bruni d'Entrecasteaux brought his two ships *Recherche* and *Espérance* to anchor in the bay. 'It will be difficult to describe my feelings at the sight of the solitary harbour situated at the extremes of the world, so perfectly enclosed that one feels separated from the rest of the universe,' he wrote.

After their storm-tossed journey from Brest via Cape Town, the ships and the 219 seamen, officers and scientists aboard recovered from scurvy and distemper at Recherche Bay. It provided fish, greens, fresh water, timber for repairs and an intriguing natural environment to study. A year later, after circumnavigating Australia, the d'Entrecasteaux expedition returned to Recherche Bay and this time met up with local Aboriginal people. The French diaries record the unfolding, friendly investigation of each other by these totally different peoples from opposite ends of the globe.

The two centuries since d'Entrecasteaux anchored in Recherche Bay have seen British colonisation, whaling stations, sawmills, coal mines, pubs and piracy all come and go. Yet as the twenty-first century dawned, the naturalness of its setting remained remarkably unchanged. Suddenly, after 2000, Tasmania's rapidly expanding export woodchip industry threatened the forest on Recherche Bay's north-east peninsula which had helped sustain the Aborigines, which had safely enfolded the French frigates in 1792, and which inspired d'Entrecasteaux's rhapsodic description.

By 2003, Recherche Bay itself needed rescue. In a race against time and government indifference, the local people, including historians, raised the alarm. Soon there were protest rallies in Hobart and a rising chorus of national and international concern.

Into the centre of this growing storm stepped Emeritus Professor John Mulvaney, Founding Professor of Prehistory at The Australian National University, and a world-renowned authority on Indigenous and cultural heritage. He had been a champion of the Franklin River and its World Heritage wilderness and archaeological sites that, against the odds, were saved from damming in 1983. His arrival at Recherche Bay lifted everyone's morale and contributed to Recherche Bay's listing as National Heritage. John Mulvaney helped trigger the vital intervention by philanthropists Dick and Pip Smith that made possible the purchase of the peninsula. That guaranteed the forest's survival as a centrepiece of the Recherche Bay region. Recherche Bay should now be incorporated into Tasmania's Wilderness World Heritage Area, which includes the Franklin River.

In *The axe had never sounded*, John Mulvaney has written the galvanising story of Recherche Bay, its Aboriginal people, the extraordinary French visits and the remarkable people and events which have followed. The book is also a tribute to John Mulvaney himself. His devotion to Australia's humanity and history was pivotal in converting the impending tragedy of Recherche Bay into a triumph for all concerned.

Senator Bob Brown
Senator for Tasmania
Leader of the Australian Greens

Foreword

Recherche Bay, north-eastern peninsula from the air, 2005. Senator Bob Brown

The north-eastern peninsula. Observatory (Bennetts) Point at bottom right; Blackswan Lagoon centre; Southport Lagoon top left, the area in which the first contact was made in 1792. Photograph by Senator Bob Brown, 2005

'The axe had never sounded'

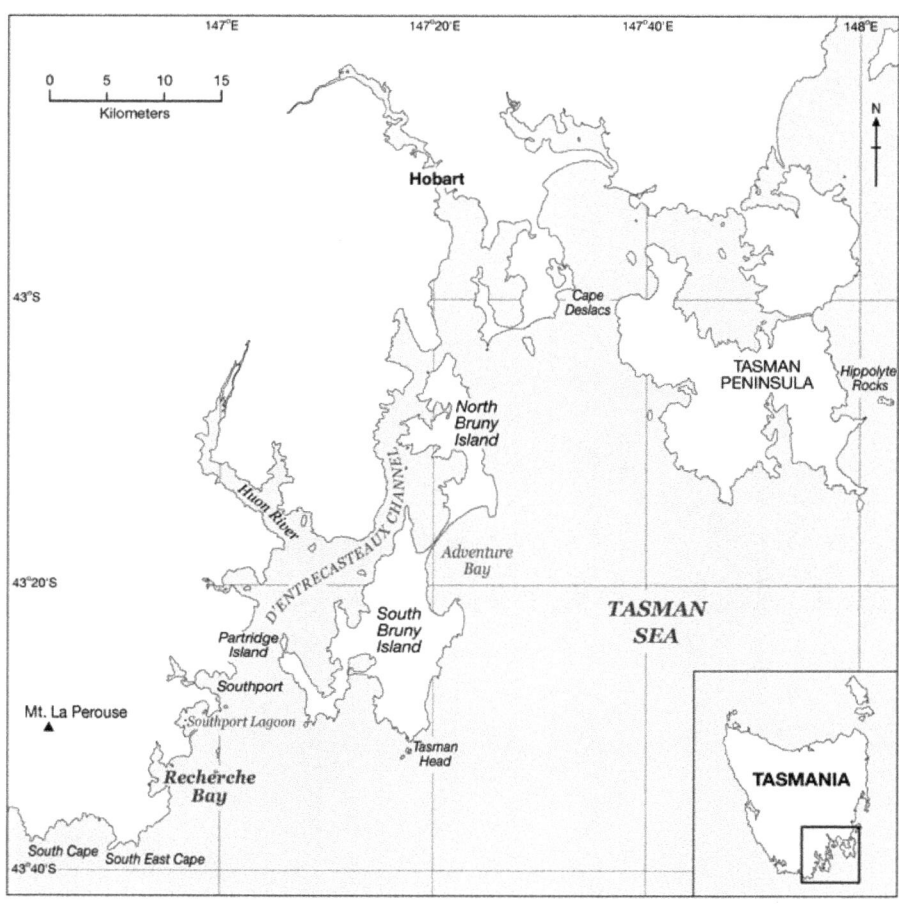

Map 1 South-eastern Tasmania

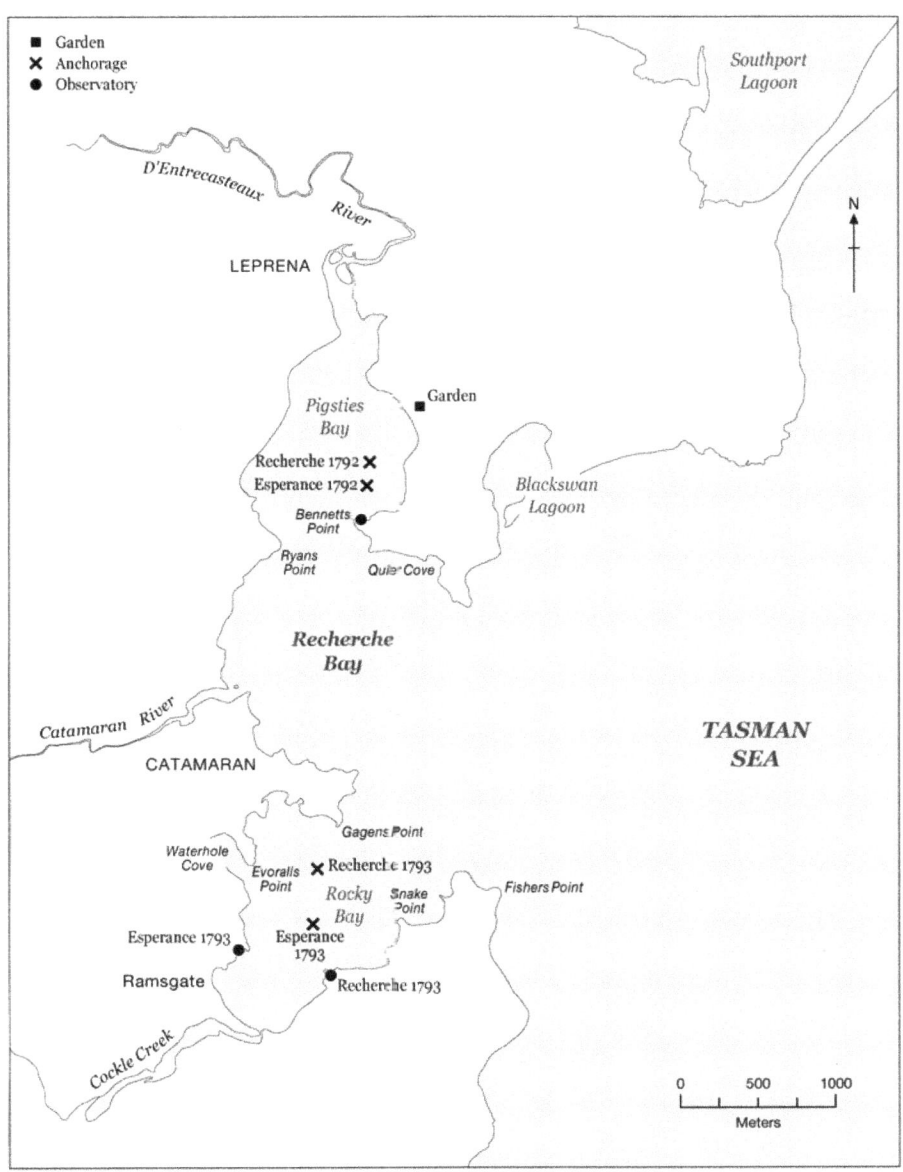

Map 2 Recherche Bay, showing places mentioned in the text

Introduction

This is a tale of two conflicting interests over a cultural landscape, between heritage conservation and political and economic expediency. Belatedly it had a happy ending. It reflects my personal involvement in heritage issues across the years, so my opinions may seem unduly on the side of heritage. For this I make no apology.

Few Australians could locate Recherche Bay on a map, while pronouncing the place 'research'. Until recently, fewer still were aware of the significant role played by French navigators in charting Australian coasts. French activities have been better appreciated since commemorative celebrations for bicentenaries of their voyaging, followed by lauding the four centuries since documented European cockleshell vessels coasted through Australian waters during 1606.

It was different a century ago, when nationalist sentiment associated with Federation simply identified history as sagas of exploration and acclaimed British achievements on sea and land. This typical message was conveyed to school children when they read Charles Long's *Stories of Australian exploration,* published in 1903 but current into the '30s when it excited (and misinformed) this schoolboy author.

British seadogs commanded the seas in Long's narrative. William Dampier merited seven pages, James Cook 18 pages, while Bass and Flinders required 28 pages. By contrast, French voyages were by-passed. D'Entrecasteaux was dismissed in two lines and Baudin received two rather derogatory paragraphs. Had Cook or Flinders reached Recherche Bay before French nationals, perhaps its modern story would have been more concerned with heritage values. The rhetoric of Prime Minister John Howard's government promotes the exploits of British heritage and peoples, so in this case it would have been unlikely to sanction the cultural and environmental vandalism proposed at Recherche Bay, which was the occasion of writing this book. As it was, this expedition memorialised the ships, officers and savants by scattering French place names in Tasmania and around the Pacific. This should surely have raised questions in Australian minds concerning the importance of the enterprise.

Recherche Bay is now a two-hour drive south from Hobart, in Tasmania's extreme south-east. Europeans first entered the Bay in 1792, although Aboriginal Tasmanians had settled southern Tasmania more than 30,000 years earlier. Vice-Admiral Bruny d'Entrecasteaux sailed his two vessels *Recherche* and *Espérance* into its sheltered waters on 23 April 1792. It proved an excellent haven for sailing ships. Huon de Kermadec,[1] captain of *Espérance* assessed it to be 'a safe and convenient port, where nature itself seems to take pleasure in assembling an infinity of resources useful to sailors who want to anchor there, whether it be for refreshing the crew after a long voyage or for repairing no matter what on the ship, even careening'.

Its entrance is delineated by peninsulas about 2.5 kilometres apart. Once inside the bay it is 7.5 kilometres from D'Entrecasteaux River at the northern end, to Cockle Creek in the south. Abundant supplies of fresh water, the navigable depth of the sea and the sandy and muddy bottom, which secured anchors, were great advantages. So was the shelving beach, which provided safe grounding for careening vessels. Testimony to the harbour's protective qualities is given by the fate of the *James Craig*, which was sunk in the late 1920s near the 1792 French anchorage. It survived for half a century until it was raised, taken to Hobart and later restored and moored near Sydney's National Maritime Museum with the Sydney Heritage Fleet.

Upon entering the harbour, d'Entrecasteaux exclaimed in his journal that: 'It will be difficult to describe my feelings at the sight of this solitary harbour situated at the extremities of the world, so perfectly enclosed that one feels separated from the rest of the universe.'[2] The area feels almost as remote today, with its dark green forest fringing much of the harbour. Although timber was selectively harvested almost a century ago, regrowth largely has replicated the scene that so impressed the French. To the west is a backdrop of rugged mountain peaks, including the frequently snow-capped Mt La Perouse, a beautiful natural monument to the failed prime objective of the d'Entrecasteaux expedition — to locate the lost La Pérouse expedition.

The frigates *Recherche* and *Espérance* sailed from Brest Harbour on 28 September 1791 in their vain search for La Pérouse, whose two ships were last seen leaving Botany Bay early in 1788. Their failure to locate the missing vessels and the disintegration of the expedition at Java during 1793 suggests a forlorn outcome for this well-equipped expedition. This was accentuated because the voyage claimed the lives of d'Entrecasteaux, his two captains, Huon de Kermadec and D'Hesmivy d'Auribeau, and many crew members.

This is the story of that ill-fated expedition, but it is focused upon its greatest success and invaluable contribution to science, navigation and the heritage of Aboriginal Tasmanians. Their two visits to Recherche Bay, in 1792 and 1793, totalled almost seven weeks. Later significant events in that harbour are also included in this story of an important place in Australian history.

Unfortunately, the second part of this story concerns the sad modern sequel. It is a tale of Federal and State ineptitude and disregard for cultural and heritage values in the interests of crass political opportunism and economic self-interest. As the nominator of a cultural landscape at Recherche Bay for registration under Commonwealth legislation as a National Heritage Place, I propose examining the saga, which involved the Tasmanian State Labor and the Commonwealth Coalition governments. Happily, the area nominated is now a registered National Heritage

Place. However, the proposed compromise solution would have ensured its destruction as an historical and cultural landscape. Then a white knight arrived on the bank floor in the person of Dick Smith who underwrote the cost of purchasing the area in dispute. I was involved in the Franklin Dam High Court case during 1982–83 and it is disappointing, even dishonourable, to find comparable rhetoric and denial or disregard of evidence repeated in this case, despite the documented evidence for its heritage significance for all Australians.

Before recounting the experiences of the d'Entrecasteaux expedition in south-east Tasmania, that exploration must be understood within the momentous and intriguing context of those years between La Pérouse's exit in 1788 and the wretched termination of the enterprise in Java during 1793. They embrace those most memorable years in French history, from rebellious mutterings to storming the Bastille, culminating in the Terror, when the guillotine ruled.

Louis XVI was alive when the expedition sailed, although the crews heard of his execution only upon their arrival in Dutch Java late in 1793; a matter of deep moment because of the divisions aboard ship between Royalists and Republicans. At that time they also had the misfortune to learn that Holland was at war with France. Although Louis XVI was virtually powerless at the time the ships sailed, he took a deep personal interest in their objectives and welfare. He wrote a long memorandum to accompany and advise d'Entrecasteaux on his voyage, solicitous of the crew's health and of the well being of any indigenous people encountered. There is a tradition that, on his way to the guillotine in 1793, Louis asked whether any news had yet been received concerning the fate of La Pérouse. The day of his execution was the date when the expedition entered Recherche Bay for its second visit.

Given the rivalry and conflict between France and England, suspicions multiplied concerning French territorial intentions in unmapped Australian waters. After all, La Pérouse followed the First Fleet into Botany Bay a few days after its arrival. Surveying activities by d'Entrecasteaux, and by Baudin seven years later, were suspected to have strategic objectives, despite their avowed scientific and humanitarian aims. This political context is crucial to appreciating international relationships.

Regardless of revolution and war during these crucial times, European cultural life flourished in this era. These years witnessed Mozart at his instrumental and operatic peak. In Austria, between 1788 and 1791, he composed the *Jupiter* and two other immortal symphonies, and his operas included *The Magic Flute*. Franz Joseph Haydn arrived in London during 1791, there to compose and conduct his symphonies 93 to 104. Over in the newly created United States, in 1789, George Washington was inaugurated as the first president. Meantime, at Port Jackson, Governor Arthur Phillip struggled to maintain a settlement and moved into Australia's first brick house in 1789.

In conformity with the alert intellectual atmosphere during the closing years of the Age of Enlightenment, scientific and geographic curiosity provided a significant mix in cultural life. While trading opportunities lurked in the background when justifying global voyaging, savants sought geographical, biological and ethnic data in the interests of learning unrelated to imperial desires. Consequently, aboard *Recherche* and *Espérance*, in addition to seamen there were men of considerable scientific, literary and artistic talent. It was this genuinely objective pursuit of knowledge that rendered this expedition so important, reflecting the purposeful sense of the age. There were 11 such savants aboard, together with two doctors and several officers of intellectual calibre. Many of them kept journals. Not all men fulfilled their potential, and three had already abandoned ship in Cape Town, but it was an exceptionally talented group that probed the potential of south-eastern Tasmania.

This story concerns the cultural landscape that is the Recherche Bay region and the fate of the investigators and collections made there. It depends upon the recent spate of publications and translations dealing with the expedition. The presumed discovery of the vegetable garden planted by the French alerted conservationists to the potential significance of the area. I have drawn freely upon Edward and Maryse Duyker's excellent translation of *Bruny D'Entrecasteaux: voyage to Australia and the Pacific* (1998) and Edward Duyker's definitive *Citizen Labillardière* (2003). Frank Horner's *Looking For La Pérouse* (1995) is a clearly written and thoughtful account. Brian Plomley and Josiane Piard-Bernier put all researchers in their debt by translating various diarists in *The General* (1993). All these authors acknowledge their debt to Hélène Richard's *Le Voyage de d'Entrecasteaux a la recherché de La Pérouse* (1986).

ENDNOTES

[1] Plomley and Piard-Bernier, *The General*, 1993: 114 – Kermadec.

[2] Duyker and Duyker (eds and trans), *Bruny d'Entrecasteaux: voyage to Australia and the Pacific*, 2001: 32.

Acknowledgements

It was Senator Bob Brown who got me involved in the fortunes of Recherche Bay. He asked me to inspect the 'garden' in February 2003, to address a protest rally in April 2005 and, a few months later, to launch his beautiful booklet portraying the peninsula from the air and a related photographic exhibition.[1] His dedicated concern proved an inspiration, not only to myself, but to his friendly group of staff and volunteers. Of these latter I owe particular thanks to Margaret Blakers and (Senator) Christine Milne.

Other Tasmanians who provided various assistance were Greg Hogg, Bruce Poulson, Deborah Wace, Wren Fraser-Cameron and our transport drivers Heather Beatie and Jane Thiele; Carl Wright provided his boat. Archaeologists Parry Kostoglou and Anne McConnell, in Hobart, and Anne Bickford and historian Edward Duyker, in Sydney, provided advice and publications. Greg Hogg and Parry Kostoglou guided me to various sites on a visit during March 2006. In Canberra, Dr Ted Lilley clarified many issues of Earth magnetism and saved me from errors, although any confusion remaining is my responsibility. Doreen Bowdery assisted in many ways. The Sydney Heritage Fleet provided images and helpful advice. The comments of referees Isabel McBryde, Michael Pearson, Michael Pickering and Kaye Price proved most valuable.

For assistance with typing (because I write with a biro) and photographic production I thank family members Michael Mulvaney (Canberra) and Mary Ramson Mulvaney (Bowral). Clare Nugent, my daughter, translated French texts.

I emphasise that critical opinions and interpretations expressed are my own and not necessarily those of the Board of *Aboriginal History* or those acknowledged above. This text was completed in April 2006 and deals with legislative changes and events only up to that date.

On advice that Tasmanian Aboriginal people prefer that term to 'Indigenous', I have used 'Aboriginal/Aborigines' throughout.

ENDNOTES
[1] Brown, 2005.

Chapter 1: Setting Out

Recherche and _Espérance_ under way. Watercolour by Frédéric Roux, Musée National de la Marine, Paris

La Recherche (petit flûte dénommée frégate) commandée par M. D'Entrcasteaux, Contre-Amiral, ayant pour conserve l'Espérance (bâtimt. de même espèze) commandée par M. Huon Kermadec, capt. de vaisseau, watercolour by Frédéric Roux, a pilot. In 'Album de Famille' de l'Amiral Willaumez. Plate 17. Musée National de la Marine, Paris [PH 169853, Cote J1102]. Note the windmills on the sterns.

La Pérouse should have sailed home to France during 1789. Despite overriding current political and revolutionary preoccupations, his absence rated highly in the national consciousness. Presumably rivalry with England over issues of global discovery and annexation, combined with trading prospects in the new lands were all factors in the situation. In this era of discovery the *Société d'Histoire Naturelle* was also concerned for the safety of scientific collections made by La Pérouse. The thrill and importance of new discoveries proved an incentive to the scientific vitality of the *Société,* just as London's Royal Society was stimulated by Cook, Bligh and other explorers. The *Société* agreed that it was urgent to locate the missing La Pérouse, so it petitioned the then ruling Constituent Assembly in Paris. On 9 February 1791, the Assembly voted affirmatively, issuing a formulaic decree to the king to dispatch a rescue mission.

Antoine-Joseph-Bruny d'Entrecasteaux, 1737-1793. National Library of Australia

Antoine-Joseph-Bruny d'Entrecasteaux, 1737–93, by Baron Etienne Hulot 1857–1918. In *Extrait du Bulletin de la Societe de Geographie* (3e trimester 1894), Paris: Societe de Geographie, 1894, p. 9. National Library of Australia

While Louis XVI was at this time a virtual prisoner and puppet, he remained forlornly dedicated to learn the fate of La Pérouse, to whom he had personally entrusted special objectives, including the need to adopt a humanitarian view towards newly found exotic peoples. Louis therefore offered enthusiastic support. It is evident that the rescue expedition was widely supported by the government, because 1,160,000 livres were made available from the French naval budget of 30 million livres.[1] Instruments and other costs brought total expenditure to 1,369,516 livres.

Antoine-Raymond-Joseph Bruny d'Entrecasteaux (1737–93) was named leader with responsibility to command two vessels to be made ready for the search and rescue expedition. The expedition was intended to combine this objective with scientific discovery and the accurate charting of unknown regions. There is no indication that land annexation was an objective. Although d'Entrecasteaux was promoted upon departure of the ships to the flag rank of rear-admiral, shipboard diarists termed him 'General', because the term admiral had not yet come into common use in France. A member of the minor nobility, d'Entrecasteaux had pursued a distinguished naval career both in war and peace since his enlistment in 1754. It culminated in 1787 with a term as Governor of Ile de France (Mauritius). He was an experienced captain and navigator, a character who commanded loyalty and a conciliator, by the time he returned to France in 1790.

During his career, the traditional control of the navy and its officer corps lay entirely with persons of noble birth or connection, entitling officers, as *gardes de la marine* to wear a conspicuous red uniform. Just before the French Revolution, in 1786, reforms introduced into the navy produced a more efficient and rational system. This included admitting officers of lower social rank, bourgeois recruits who usually were merchant marine officers who transferred to the navy. A midshipman with six years service might also join officer ranks following an examination. Such newly recruited officers wore blue uniforms, a reminder of their more lowly social status.

Although the Constituent Assembly integrated these two officer branches in October 1789, it became a significant irritant during the expedition because of rivalry between the 'red' officers — traditional royal loyalists — and the 'blue' officers — most of whom were republicans. Testimony to the respect in which officers and crew held d'Entrecasteaux is that he had no major disciplinary problems. Many naval vessels in those years faced difficulties with revolutionary-stimulated ill discipline. This was particularly the case with crews drawn from Brest, where a mutiny occurred during 1790. This expedition was fitted out and crewed at Brest.

The Officers

D'Entrecasteaux was given freedom to select his own officers and he recruited several men who had served under him and in whose capabilities he trusted; their uniforms were red. As this book concerns Recherche Bay rather than the entire voyaging, only those persons who contributed to events there are discussed.

To captain *Espérance*, d'Entrecasteaux turned to his former experienced first lieutenant and friend, Jean-Michel Huon de Kermadec (1748–93), who was promoted to the rank of flag-captain. Unfortunately, Kermadec, at 43 the oldest officer, was already in poor health and, though a man of rough humour, was physically weak and irresolute at times. Yet he was trusted by d'Entrecasteaux,

'The axe had never sounded'

sent to Brest with the tasks of supervising the remodelling of two ships for expedition requirements, provisioning the vessels and recruiting their crews. Consequently, the Breton region supplied most of the men. At this period, while crewmen had medical examinations, officers were exempt. Kermadec was not the only officer who would never have sailed had he been examined medically, and the voyage cost him his life.

Another favoured officer known to d'Entrecasteaux was Elisabeth-Paul-Edouard de Rossel (1765–1829) who, when a senior midshipman, had shown promise in making nautical observations. Aged only 26, he was an excellent choice and a vital member of the expedition. Rossel was destined to become ultimate commander of the expedition and its chief astronomer. In later life, Rossel became the distinguished head of the French *Bureau des Longitudes* and editor of his late captain's journal. A royalist sympathiser, a contemporary described him as 'a little man as round as a barrel,' ugly, gentle and cheerful.[2]

When d'Entrecasteaux governed Ile de France, Alexis-Ignace de Crestin (1763–94) was his aide-de-camp; he was invited to join him again as a lieutenant. Jean-Baptiste-Philibert Willaumez (1793–1843) also served previously under d'Entrecasteaux as an ensign, the title then given to sub-lieutenants who were promoted from the lower deck. Despite his republicanism, d'Entrecasteaux's trust was justified by his valuable contribution. Willaumez, then 28, rose to be a vice-admiral and, despite his republicanism, a count.

Another recruit known to be reliable was Alexandre-François de le Fresnaye de Saint-Aignan (1768–1849) who added violin playing to his naval capabilities. While his music was appreciated on board, his fiddle was to irritate Aboriginal Tasmanians. When the vessels departed, lieutenants Rossel, Crestin, Willaumez and Saint-Aignan all sailed on the *Recherche*, with d'Entrecasteaux.

Command of *Recherche* went to an officer not known to d'Entrecasteaux, but who came highly recommended. Alexandre d'Hesmivy d'Auribeau (1760–94) was promoted flag-captain during the voyage. An unfortunate choice, he was an extremely haughty royalist, belonging to a noble Provencal family. He proved a capable sailor and a sound observer of Aborigines, but his arrogant personality encouraged personality clashes at sea and it was to have serious implications for the expedition's termination in Java. He also suffered chronic ill health, which should have disqualified his participation. There is some belief that he also took drugs.

On *Espérance*, commanded by Kermadec, one of the lieutenants had also served under d'Entrecasteaux. This was Claude-Marie-Dominique de la Grandière (1767–95). He should not be confused with his shipmate, 19-year-old Julien de la Gravière (1772–1849), who wrote a private and unpublished account of the voyage, which was used by his son, in 1860, to write a life of his father. Both father and son rose to admiral rank. Lieutenant Trobriand, aged 26, proved a reliable officer and later served practically in command of *Espérance* due to his Captain's illness.

Also aboard *Espérance* was sub-lieutenant Jacques-Malo La Motte du Portail (1761–1812). A staunch royalist, yet a former merchant marine officer, he became soured because he was not promoted to the rank he desired. His jaundiced version of ship life provides helpful insights into daily routine. In particular, a series of letters that he wrote survived, although they were never sent to his supposed fiancée, Zélie. There are doubts as to whether Zélie even existed, because this may have been his secretive means of frank journal keeping that would not risk confiscation. If so, he succeeded, because most officers were forced to surrender their journals at the voyage end, in Java.

The youth of officers is a striking feature of the crews. Except for Kermadec, the age of officers on both ships ranged between Jurien, aged 19, and d'Auribeau, aged 31. Several men in their mid-20s performed admirably when responsibility was thrust upon them through illness, death or opportunities to explore. Rossel assumed command at 28 years of age.

The Savants

The naval captains and officers had to adapt to both crowded quarters and mostly bourgeois civilians appointed as scientists (termed naturalists). As civilians, these men were not subject to naval laws and regulations, although they claimed privileges similar to the officers. Understandably, their purpose lay in discovery and collecting on land, so their concerns frequently conflicted with those of the officers whose function was with the ocean and its weather, tides and timetable. The scientists always desired more time to explore, the sailors to up-anchor. A further likely cause of friction developed between the mostly royalist officers and the naturalist intellectuals, the majority of whom were republicans. These factors became evident at Recherche Bay and were later to have serious consequences on Java.

D'Entrecasteaux was well aware of the problems of sailing with civilians. Having experienced friction aboard en route to Cape Town, he wrote to his Minister on 13 February 1792 expressing his feelings and annoyance as a naval officer:

> nothing is more harmful to an expedition of this kind than to employ resources foreign to the service, for [naturalists] come with extraordinary pretensions. Ignorance of the regulations makes them think they are being submitted to humiliating treatment; boredom and the idleness of shipboard life makes them unsettled, suspicious and inclined to foment troubles.[3]

Such incidents and tensions also worked both ways. At Cape Town, the chief astronomer, an artist, and the mineralogist disembarked to return home.

'The axe had never sounded'

Jacques-Julien Houton de Labillardière. National Library of Australia

Jacques-Julien Houton de Labillardière. In *The literature of Australian birds: a history and a bibliography of Australian ornithology*, Hubert Massey Whittell, Perth: Paterson Brokensha, 1954, Plate 23. National Library of Australia

Given the rudimentary state of scientific disciplines at this period and the limited expertise for investigating new lands amongst the scientific group, those men recommended by the *Société d' Histoire Naturelle* possessed qualifications of some potential and their activities justified their inclusion. The unfortunate loss of some collections and the confiscation of their journals negated the work of some naturalists, through no fault of their own.

The oldest, most senior and most vexatious scientist was Jacques-Julien Houton de Labillardière (1755–1834), who conveniently and, as a republican, democratically chose simply to be called Labillardière. Born into a provincial middle class Normandy family, he studied medicine at Montpellier, Reims and Paris. However, he became a botanist of repute, with field experience in Europe and Syria. For two years he lived in London, where he studied the plants brought back by James Cook. Fortunately for his future career, he met Sir Joseph Banks while in England. He was a person of strong convictions and it is testimony to d'Entrecasteaux's tolerant command that only one incident, discussed later, is known of his firmly disputing Labillardière's demands.

Louis-August Deschamps (1755–1842) and Claude-Antoine Gaspard Riche (1762–97) also took medical degrees before moving into natural science. Their division of duties was determined by d'Entrecasteaux only when they were at Amboina, following the first visit to Recherche Bay. Labillardière was undisputed in the botanical field, Riche took birds, shells and worms, while Deschamps was responsible for mammals, fish, amphibians and insects. In the absence of a mineralogist, Deschamps also assumed that duty.

Louis Ventenat (1765–94) was a priest, originally chaplain and confessor to d'Entrecasteaux, who later banished him to the *Espérance* for possibly encouraging insubordination below decks (he was a republican in sentiment).[4] As an enlisted naval person he was subject to naval rules, which also meant that he did not receive as much remuneration as the naturalists were paid. He proved to be a conscientious and thoughtful assistant botanist. Ventenat possessed a sense of humour. Admitting that he and Riche got themselves lost on occasion, he wryly observed, 'Mr Deschamps was never in this predicament; he took care always to be on board for breakfast, dinner and supper.'[5] Indeed, Deschamps contributed least of all to the savants on the voyage and in the end his collections and journal became lost during his return voyage to France in 1803. His ship was captured by the Royal Navy and his collections were seized.

Riche belonged to a Lyons district legal family who achieved high medical results. As he was a consumptive, the voyage may have been taken as a health cure. A republican of conviction, he travelled on the *Espérance*. Labillardière and Deschamps were shipmates on *Recherche*, but there any similarity ceases. Labillardière was an impatient explorer, spending undue time on the land to the commander's annoyance. Royalist Deschamps hailed from St Omer, near Calais, and chose to remain aboard ship much of the time available for fieldwork.

Industrious Felix Delahaye (1767–1829) was engaged as gardener-botanist, following enthusiastic recommendations from the head of the celebrated Paris botany school, *Jardin du Roi*, soon to be renamed *Jardin des Plantes*, where he worked. He arrived in Brest with four cases of garden seeds, one of fruit tree nuts, one containing gardening tools and another gardener's clothing. His activities and dedication surely merited status ranking with the naturalists, but the unfortunate man, who was to play a central role in determining the heritage fortunes of Recherche Bay, was exiled to eat and sleep in the fetid crew's quarters. The Bligh of France, he took breadfruit plants to Mauritius.

Astronomical observations were to have been the responsibility of Abbé Claude Bertrand (1755–92). His intrepid spirit seemed assured, because in 1784 he ascended in a balloon, only one year after the first airborne balloon. His reputation commanded the highest remuneration of 3,000 livres per annum, whereas most naturalists received 2,400 livres; lowly Delahaye's annual salary was only 1,000 livres, although he received compensation of 1,236 livres for his practical equipment.

Much to everyone's gratification, Bertrand abandoned the expedition at Cape Town because his health and character proved unacceptable for a long, crowded voyage. A Benedictine chaplain, Don Ambroise Pierson (1765–94) assisted conscientiously in the essential astronomical work. In Bertrand's absence, however, it was Lieutenant Rossel who distinguished himself in the astronomical field, together with measuring terrestrial magnetism at various latitudes. When he later published the d'Entrecasteaux journal, he added considerable detail concerning the astronomical record. He received enthusiastic astronomical assistance, also, from Willaumez and an 18-year-old midshipman, Achard de Bonvouloir.

An important objective of the expedition was to chart unknown coastlines. In hydrography and cartography, new international standards in accuracy were set by Charles-François Beautemps-Beaupré (1766–1854), and nowhere better than in Tasmanian waters. Aged only 25, he applied new techniques of surveying, described later. This was the beginning of a career that made him a Grand Officer of the Legion of Honour. He sailed on *Recherche*.

Like Miroir-Jouvency (ca 1754–98) aboard *Espérance*, Beautemps-Beaupré was termed a geographer in the parlance of that time, but surveyors and cartographers they both were. Miroir-Jouvency had the prior experience of mapping Corsica but, although active, his role was less productive than that of the ever busy Beautemps-Beaupré.

Each vessel carried an artist, but only one of them sailed beyond Cape Town. This was Jean Piron, about whom little is known and many of whose drawings were lost. He befriended Labillardière and explored Recherche Bay with him. Fortunately, he presented copies of some drawings, including those of Tasmanian people, to his friend. Consequently, Labillardière included them as illustrations in his book, published in 1800. In this way, priceless visual records were preserved of French contacts with the Tasmanians. That he portrayed them according to the rubrics of classical art is less important than that he depicted them sympathetically as friendly and fully human people, indicating that their stoicism derived from the hard life they had, as opposed to the 'soft' primitivism of Polynesians.

There was one crew member aboard the *Recherche* whose presence attracts modern media attention and gossipy surmises. This was the steward, Louis Girardin, actually Louise (1754–94), the only female on the expedition.[6] Her disguise was maintained throughout, even to fighting a duel that resulted in her receiving a wounded arm. Even so, her slight figure and facial appearance made her suspect, although the fact that d'Entrecasteaux provided her with a tiny separate cabin assisted greatly in her deception.

Louise clearly could look after herself, despite taunts from suspicious crew. From a bourgeois family — her father was a Versailles wine merchant — she was a youthful-looking 38 years old. She had been widowed, then borne an illegitimate child to a lover who deserted her. Fleeing from her wrathful father, she was assisted by a widowed sister of Kermadec, presumably a former Versailles friend. She coaxed Kermadec to give her a place in the crew of the ship he then commanded. When a mutiny threatened, he had her transferred to the *Recherche*.

Surely d'Entrecasteaux knew her secret, but there is no evidence that she granted sexual favours to anyone. Even the cynical and forthright La Motte du Portail told Zélie, that 'we did not really have anything positive on which to ground our suspicion, and our suspicions were based only on the way this person was built'.[7] Whatever the gossip concerning Louise, her presence must have provoked many tensions and subjects for coarse discussion on the voyage. She remained undetected until her death in Java.

There was one other person in the crew about whom only one passing reference has been found. In writing his official report of a boat journey on 20 May 1792, Lieutenant Saint Aignan reported that his team included Crestin, three men 'and the little cabinboy Hypolite'. French naval vessels carried a number of cabinboys, termed 'mousse'. This lad presumably was Charles-Francois-Hipolite Deslacs d'Arcambal (1777–1805), of Parisian aristocratic birth who died at Trafalgar. Cape Deslacs, which they surveyed while he was in the boat, was presumably named in his honour. It is west of the Tasman Peninsula. The Hippolyte rocks, east of that peninsula may have a similar origin. The rocks were known by that name when Baudin sailed past in 1802.[8] So this 15-year-old lad's name is remembered today, while places named for many senior shipmates were replaced by British nomenclature.

It is noteworthy that when the ships sailed from Brest, all but two of the *Recherche* officers had served previously under d'Entrecasteaux, who had chosen them for this enterprise. The companion vessel was commanded by his friend Kermadec, to whom he entrusted the vital task of equipping and victualling the expedition. Within contemporary standards, most of the naturalists and geographers were well qualified and they received the approval of French scientific societies. This should have proven a harmonious and successful voyage, yet it ended in death and disaster, while La Pérouse was never found. At Recherche Bay, however, its scientific achievements were of global significance, while interaction between sailors and Tasmanians proved a model of mutual respect and observation.

The crews were recruited largely from the revolutionary Brest area, so while many officers were loyal to the king, most Breton seamen would have held republican sentiments. The vessels therefore reflected a microcosm of French revolutionary society, so it points to the diplomatic control exerted by d'Entrecasteaux that he kept shipboard order. For the mostly republican savants, their departure from France in those revolutionary times combined with the anticipation of discoveries. Wordsworth's celebrated lines (*The Prelude*, Book 2, lines 108-9) are appropriate to their emotions:

> Bliss it was that dawn to be alive,
> But to be young was very heaven

Ships and Stores

In the Captain Cook tradition, preference was given to solid roomy craft for the expedition. Naval storeships (*gabare*) were chosen, the same class as La Pérouse's two vessels, *l'Astrolobe* and *La Boussole*. The selected ships originally were named *Truite* and *Duranse*. The former, a four year old vessel, was imaginatively renamed *Recherche*, while the second ship became *Espérance* (Hope). This latter was built 10 years earlier and it proved tediously slow. Both craft were comparable in size and were reclassified as frigates (ironically implying swiftness). *Recherche* measured 114 by 26 feet (34.7m x 8m). Earlier sources gave their tonnage as 500, but following a critical appraisal of their measurements by Frank Horner, his more reliable estimate made their tonnage closer to 350.[9] This means that they were comparable in size to Cook's *Endeavour* and Flinders' *Investigator*, much smaller than a true frigate.

Vessels of this type were crewed normally by 60 sailors, but due to their special requirements each now required capacity for 110 persons. In an attempt to save deck space (and, incidentally, showing their peaceful intentions) most cannon were removed. Three 8-pounders remained on either side of the gundeck, while two of the recently developed close-range 20-pounder carronades were added. On both ships this armament was cluttered and confined by pens holding six sheep and 50 fowls. Added armament on each ship included 45 muskets, 35 pistols, 130 battle-axes and 50 swords.[10]

On each vessel provision had to made for extra accommodation and stores. This was met by constructing an orlop deck below the lower deck. This divided the deep hold in half, to which meagre light and ventilation came through three hatches. Cabins were crammed into any available deck spaces, while the captains occupied special quarters built on the quarterdeck. The great cabin across the stern served multiple functions — as the mess for officers and scientists, a meetings area, and a much disputed working place for the naturalists. As for the crew, they socialised on deck in the confined space beside the long boats. Iron galleys instead of brick cooking galleys were installed. Each ship had a small corn-grinding windmill installed above the poop deck. Little bread was baked from the flour, however, as one mill soon toppled during a storm.

For voyaging into the unknown, the hulls required strengthening against grounding or damage and it was becoming customary to attach thin copper sheeting, whose smoothness assisted speed and offered protection against worms and barnacles. An alternative solution was necessary in the event that this protection needed to be replaced, as copper would be unavailable in remote lands. This solution was a double hull of pinewood into which flat-headed nails were hammered so closely together that they virtually presented an unbroken metal surface. An ingenious solution, but at a cost, because the surface was not as smooth as copper sheeting, so the nails served to slow the ship and encourage weed growth.

Kermadec was instructed to secure only good quality rations, although in this task the future proved that dishonest provisioners ignored him. When opened on the high seas, many stores were stale and weevil infested. During the late eighteenth century the staple French seaman's monotonous ration amounted to a daily issue of 600 grams of bread or biscuit, fresh or salted meat or cod, cheese and dried or pickled vegetables. Sometimes special items were provided, such as soup tablets, butter and coffee. In theory this provided about 4,000 calories daily, a diet superior to that of most peasants ashore, although it was seriously deficient in vitamin C. Naval officers received a monetary table allowance, so they brought their own rations, or purchased food and drink at ports of call. Naturalists followed the same practice.[11]

Then there were liquid supplies. Water required regular replenishment, but alcohol proved less available to explorers. An indication of French thirst was provided by Bougainville's voyage to the Pacific during the 1760s. His crew of 200 drew upon 50,000 litres of water and 60,000 litres of wine and brandy.

Scurvy posed the critical sea voyaging problem of the era. Sailors succumbed to unaccountable lassitude and debility due to vitamin C deficiency (ascorbic acid). Swollen and bleeding gums, loosened teeth, stiffness in joints and anaemia followed. It was believed that antidotes were sauerkraut and vinegar, or citrus fruit. Consequently, the expedition carried lemon rob, a syrup made from boiled lemons. Unfortunately, the boiling process probably destroyed the essential vitamin C, robbing the rob of much value. Everybody at that time deferred to Captain James Cook's wisdom, so they relied upon quantities of malt extract, a residue from brewing, which he favoured, served as spruce beer. Modern opinion is that Cook erred. Malt extract lacked vitamin C, so it was not antiscorbutic.

A decade later — too late to save lives on the d'Entrecasteaux expedition — Nicolas Baudin found a partial solution. His crew had suffered severely on the voyage to Sydney. In 1802, he pursued library research in Sydney, due to the courtesy of Governor King. He consulted 35 narratives of voyaging and determined that scurvy became serious only when ships exceeded 60 to 70 days at sea between ports. So he wisely put into port more frequently and took lime juice aboard, proving the correctness of his deductions. The d'Entrecasteaux vessels frequently exceeded the 60 days rule. Baudin's research was shown to be valid only in 1986. Clinical trials in USA proved that the store of vitamin C in a human body disappears within 68 to 90 days.[12]

ENDNOTES

[1] Plomley and Piard-Bernier, *The General*, 1993: 4. The information on individuals and ships in this chapter is drawn from Horner, 1995 and Duyker, 2003.

[2] Duyker, *Citizen Labillardière*, 2003: 70.

[3] Horner, *Looking for La Pérouse*, 1995: 57.

[4] Duyker and Duyker (eds and trans), *Bruny d'Entrecasteaux: voyage to Australia and the Pacific*, 2001: 339.

[5] Plomley and Piard-Bernier, *The General*, 1993: 354 – Ventenat.

[6] Plomley and Piard-Bernier, *The General*, 1993: 340 – du Portail; Duyker, *Citizen Labillardière*, 2003: 293 n.63.

[7] Plomley and Piard-Bernier, *The General*, 1993: 340.

[8] Duyker and Duyker (eds and trans), *Bruny d'Entrecasteaux: voyage to Australia and the Pacific*, 2001: 340 n.21; Plomley and Piard-Bernier, *The General*, 1993: 127 – Saint Aignan; Cornell, *The journal of Post Captain Nicolas Baudin*, 1974: 408.

[9] Horner, *Looking for La Pérouse*, 1995: 26, 274.

[10] Labillardière, *Voyage in search of La Pérouse*, 1800: 18.

[11] Taillemite, in Hardy and Frost, *European voyaging*, 1990: 57-60.

[12] Watt, in Hardy and Frost, *European voyaging*, 1990: 51-2; Guicheteau and Kernéis, 1990: 67; Estensen, *The life of George Bass*, 2005: 12.

Chapter 2: Recherche Bay

With an easterly breeze facilitating their departure from Brest, the frigates sailed on 21 September 1791. There was immediate excitement aboard *Recherche*, when three stowaways caused d'Entrecasteaux to order a return to shore. They were unlucky. Three further stowaways emerged too late to be offloaded, so they joined the crew.

The vessels reached Cape Town 15 weeks out of Brest. Sailing again from Cape Town on 16 February 1792, they acquired two further stowaways.[1] 66 days later they concluded that Adventure Bay was near. English seafarers including James Cook and William Bligh favoured the shelter of Adventure Bay, on Bruny Island, because of the opportunities there for replenishing water, wood and fish resources. The area was then assumed to form part of Tasmania's mainland, until d'Entrecasteaux proved that it was an island. Bligh was making use of Adventure Bay's natural facilities for HMS *Providence* when the French were at Cape Town, during February 1792.

Sailing before the winds in the stormy roaring forties, conditions proved unduly rough on 14 April, when a huge wave washed over *Recherche*. Water poured down onto the orlop deck and the hold. It swamped Labillardière's cabin, while a further wave flung d'Entrecasteaux against the writing desk in his cabin, breaking a rib. Bruised and sore, he was confined to his bunk for several days and was not on deck to contribute his experience and navigational sense when it was needed.

Through a major compass-bearing error the French were about to make their most significant geographical and scientific discovery, the D'Entrecasteaux Channel and Aboriginal Tasmanians. On 21 April, the lookout sighted the two rocky marine navigational guideposts, the pinnacles of the Mewstone and Eddystone, rising above the stormy ocean south of Tasmania. Now almost seven months out of Brest, short of water and wood and beyond the 60-day scurvy threshold, all hands eagerly anticipated landfall. What followed has alternative explanations, though human error played the crucial role.

Willaumez took the *Recherche*'s bearings on 21 April. At 12.29pm, Eddystone bore S41° E, at 12.34pm that pinnacle was S35° E, but at 1pm Willaumez measured S19° W. Such a reading was impossible, but it went unchallenged by Rossel who was on the quarter-deck. This is the version of the mistake mentioned by most diarists. In fairness to Rossel and others concerned, possibly they were preoccupied because coastal conditions were hazy and the British charts available provided minimal detail on this dimly viewed and unknown coast. Assisted by the false compass reading they concluded that what they discerned through the mist was Tasman Head on Bruny Island. Probably they were near South Cape, followed by South East Cape, on Tasmania's mainland some 40 kilometres west of Tasman Head. Tolerant and injured d'Entrecasteaux (or possibly as written by Rossel who edited the admiral's journal), made no reference to this error.[2] Even the prestige of James Cook helped to mislead them. La Motte du Portail informed Zélie: 'We were skirting the coast with Cook's maps in our hands, all of us more convinced of the exactitude of his work.'[3]

On *Espérance* meantime, the officers knew that Tasman Head was further east, so they were surprised when *Recherche* turned northwards and headed into what Tasman, in 1642, had named Storm Bay and which subsequent captains had avoided. In reality they were entering the D'Entrecasteaux Channel, with *Espérance* obediently following into those uncharted waters. Assuming that they were entering a bay they sailed on seeking a haven. They had to anchor before dusk, in 14 fathoms over a usefully sandy bottom. Two headlands were visible from the anchorage and St Aignan was sent in a ship's boat to reconnoitre the situation. He returned to confirm that the headlands marked the entrance to a good harbour. Meanwhile, sailors spent their time energetically fishing, hauling in a substantial catch as a welcome dietary change. In this accidental manner Recherche Bay became known to Europeans.

Recherche Bay entrance from Bennetts Point, 2003. John Mulvaney

Recherche Bay entrance from Bennetts Point. John Mulvaney, 2003

Communication between the two anchored ships was facilitated when du Portail was rowed across from *Espérance* and spoke with the injured commander in his cabin. Possibly d'Entrecasteaux was relieved to find a suitable harbour, because he was in a generous mood. He informed Portail that he was immediately promoted to lieutenant's rank, confirmed with 'a kiss from Mons d'Auribeau'. Portail was not alone in his good fortune, as three others were promoted to ensign rank.[4]

Under calm conditions the following morning both vessels were safely towed by invigorated oarsmen into the bay. They anchored in the northern sector, later termed the Port du Nord, or 'little bay', today the unimaginative Pig Sties Bay. They moored over 100 metres from the beach north of Bennetts Point; *Recherche* lay some 70 metres north of *Espérance*. Gazing at this pristine landscape, Labillardière voiced the ethos of noble nature: 'We were filled with admiration at the sight of these ancient forests, in which the sound of the axe had never been heard.'[5] Turning his eyes towards the harbour, he exclaimed with exaggerated praise that 'more than 100 vessels of the line might ride here with safety'. D'Entrecasteaux felt equally emotional: 'With every step, one encounters the beauties of unspoilt nature ... trees reaching a very great height ... are devoid of branches along the trunk, but crowned with an everlasting green foliage. Some of these trees seem as ancient as the world'. Little wonder that in this peaceful Eden, d'Entrecasteaux rapidly improved in health and was reported completely restored within a few days.[6] Matthew Flinders paid him an unreserved compliment, when he praised the discovery of this harbour as 'the most important discovery which has been made in [Tasmania] from the time of Tasman'.[7]

During the 24 days spent moored in the harbour, 200 men were set to work as ships and shore became a hive of activity. It was a welcome break from shipboard routine, although a busy one as most of the crews worked ashore. Before describing the scientific research, it is appropriate to note these various activities, many of which must have left archaeological traces on land or seabed. The example of the preservation of the *James Craig* over a century later, is a reminder that archaeological evidence of this visit may be preserved in the mud and sand. D'Entrecasteaux provided testimony to the constitution of the seabed when they had difficulty in raising an anchor which was 'too deeply buried in the mire'. 'With this type of seafloor,' he concluded, 'where the anchors sink to the point of disappearing, it is necessary to raise the anchor frequently.'[8]

'The axe had never sounded'

Looking towards Mt La Perouse from the 1792 beach, 2003. John Mulvaney

View west from the 1792 beach towards Mt La Perouse. John Mulvaney, 2003

The harbour swarmed with fish and seamen commenced an active harvest, catching so many fish by line and net that a prime task was to dry the surplus which was not immediately cooked and eaten. As they departed the harbour, the log of *Espérance* wryly reported 'there was so much fish hanging out to dry that we presented a truly magnificent sight sailing off ... decked out with garlands of fish!'[9]

Officers under d'Auribeau's direction selected the sandy beach and the area behind Bennetts Point for erecting tents and for industrial activities, which went on alongside the tents erected for astronomical observations. For efficient control, all activities were set close together. There were two forges for metal working. One of the urgent tasks was to reforge a broken link in an anchor chain. Charcoal was essential for cooking in the galleys, so kilns were constructed for wood burning to produce charcoal. An area was delimited for washing linen. The personal washing needs of the crews were encouraged by each person receiving a ration of one and a half pounds of soap; every fourth day, time was allowed for personal clothes washing. Sailors also bathed in the sea for their own cleanliness. As it was well into autumn, and Labillardière reported that snow increased on the mountains, the cool water was unlikely to have attracted all crew members. However, Labillardière reported that sailors 'bathed here very frequently' and he expressed relief that nobody was taken by a shark.[10]

With so many men ashore pursuing different tasks, it was necessary to recall them in an organised manner. Each day at 6.30pm a red flag was hoisted on the mainmast of each ship and oared boats were sent to collect the men.

A repair yard was constructed for the ship's oared boats, which had proved unsuitable. They had so little freeboard that their load capacity was small and cargo was in danger of being swamped. One boat from *Recherche* capsized at the harbour entrance. It proved necessary to add height to the gunwales through the addition of washboards to both the 12-ton dinghy and to the smaller boats. D'Auribeau referred to 'very extensive repairs, especially to the oared boats which had to be pulled up on the shore so as to raise their sides, a long and delicate operation in a place where the timber was of very bad quality for this purpose'. Lieutenant Trobriand was so dismissive of the boats that he said that they were more suited to be 'hung in churches'. Searching amongst these unknown tree species, the carpenters cut down various trees in hope some would provide useful timber. They were frustrated because so much timber proved rotten inside the trunk. According to Labillardière, blue gum, the newly discovered species, which he named *Eucalyptus globules*, answered best to their requirements.[11]

Today there is a large dry-stone structure with a straight side located behind Bennetts Point that requires archaeological investigation. It is constructed from carefully laid rocks some 20 metres long and one metre high. Some claim that it represents the base structure of the observatory. But this is unlikely, as discussed later. It may have served for the repair of the boats. A surveyed plan dated 1863 indicates that at this date there were three huts situated at this location, together with a 'craft' in full sail, but firmly placed on land.[12] It may indicate boat repair being carried out which utilised the stone structure. It surely required many hands to carry and lay so many rocks. Until excavations establish the origin of this considerable platform, it is presumed that the French sailors constructed it and that it was expanded and utilised for boat repairs then, and half a century later, when whaling boats were based in the harbour. Two boats were built here during the late 1850s. It may be relevant that the crew came mainly from Brittany, a centre of dry-stone walling.

Meantime, the shallow sandy tidal stretch allowed the safe beaching of the frigates, so that they tilted on their sides, or careened, to allow cleaning and caulking of their hulls. Another major task was required to fill the many casks with fresh water. Water was abundantly available in streams around the bay, but some proved brackish, while others could not be approached by the long boat that ferried the heavy casks to the ships. Consequently, attempts to utilise some sources were abandoned and the main water supply was established on the western shore. This situation necessitated men to stand in the water while a cask filled, then manhandle it out to the longboat and lift it aboard. Prudently, given the surplus of good drinking water, any empty wine casks also were filled.[13]

Axes were certainly now heard in the forests, as axemen collected wood for charcoal production and dry wood for future use in the galley fires. A large quantity of wood was stowed in the hold. All needs were met, although the charcoal burners produced only 15 sacks of charcoal, less than anticipated from the quantity of wood burned.[14]

The enigmatic stone structure at Bennetts Point, 2003. John Mulvaney

The enigmatic stone structure at Bennetts Point, approximately 20m x 1m high. Was it constructed in 1792 upon which to repair the rowing boats, or was it made by boat builders during the 1850s? Photograph by John Mulvaney, 2004

Upon their arrival in the harbour, a boat was provided for Beautemps-Beaupré and Crestin, with orders to map the harbour and sound its depths. A precise and accurate chart resulted from their effort. Revised during the 1793 visit, it was reproduced in Labillardière's book published in 1800. Less productivity resulted from the misguided enthusiasm of Lieutenant Le Grand, a keen fisherman. He convinced Kermadec that he could put to good use the whaleboat purchased in Cape Town. He advocated that it be rowed out of the harbour and a few hundred metres north. There it should be manhandled across a sandspit of some 120 metres to launch on Blackswan Lagoon, where an abundant catch of fish would result. The lagoon was surrounded by marshy vegetation, which rendered net fishing impossible, so two days were wasted and the boat put at risk of damage.[15]

During their entire stay, the French noticed smoke from Aboriginal fires and, in local travels through the forest, brush shelters and hearths and food remains were observed, but the people evaded them, although they must have watched them keenly. Prejudices died hard for seaman Ladroux. Even though they encountered no Aborigines, hostile or friendly, during the first visit, he complained: 'you don't know whether these savages eat each other and it is possible that they want to crunch us up because instead of coming near us they stay out of the way'. On one occasion, men under Le Danseur, pilot on *Espérance*, came upon a recently abandoned campfire, which they soon rekindled. Le Danseur left his knife in reciprocity for the fire's use. The ship's log wryly recorded: 'he knew [the knife] not much good, but if he did, after all he would get a better one'.[16]

That same log entry included a reference of modern relevance. Noting that strong wind agitated the trees, but that they sheltered the moorings, the sage advice was as follows: 'If Europeans come out here, they would be well advised not to cut any trees, which are great protection against the wind.'[17]

Recherche Bay, revisited summer 1793

Having traversed the South Pacific in a vain search for La Pérouse, the ships sailed west through Indonesia and down the Australian west coast. There they surveyed the Recherche Archipelago and Esperance harbour, a seemingly barren area. *Espérance* was down to its last 10 barrels of water, so the frigates used the westerly wind to return to the familiar and welcome facilities of Recherche Bay.

Espérance, now desperately short of water, sailed ahead of *Recherche*. On 21 January 1793 they entered the Bay, but unfavourable winds made entry impossible into their former northern anchorage. Kermadec headed for the southern arm, their Bay du Sud, or Bay of Rocks, today's Rocky Bay. He found suitable moorings without any difficulty, although he had no chart of this area. The *Recherche* officers, particularly d'Auribeau, favoured returning to their original anchorage, but Kermadec gave confident assurances that conditions were good in this southern harbour. When *Recherche* headed towards the southern area (equipped with Beautemps-Beaupré's chart) they grounded. Even with the pulling power of oared boats from both vessels, they remained firmly stuck for three hours. To add insult to the indignant d'Auribeau, it was found that the gushing streams of last year were dry. Fortunately for calm on the quarter deck, a boat party soon located an abundant and accessible water source on the western shore at Waterhole Cove. Even so, d'Entrcasteaux, probably prompted by the doubting d'Auribeau, insisted that the latter and the chief surgeon first inspect the water supply before they made the final decision to anchor. The water proved of good quality, although the last word was with d'Auribeau, who declared that its taste was reedy.[18]

'The axe had never sounded'

Upon reflection, when writing at the conclusion of their three weeks sojourn, d'Auribeau relented. He observed that:

> The Bay of Rocks offers an extremely good anchorage where one finds great depth in several places. Moreover, the holding there is very good and one can be at ease in regard to the safety of the ship. Entrance and exit are easy when both are made with a suitable wind. The stream that we found there is all that one could wish for; water can be taken easily and is of good quality.[19]

The familiar routine of the previous visit was followed through the following 21 days. Land base was established at the head of Rocky Bay, adjacent to Cockle Creek and the *Espérance* observatory on the shore further to the east. The flat land around this 'good sized stream', allowed for compact arrangement and supervision of shore installations. Its water, nowhere near the drinking water source, therefore provided fine opportunities for washing clothes. Hay was collected to feed the shipboard goats. All empty barrels were filled and the cooper prudently repaired a number, ensuring the maximum supply aboard. Firewood was readily collected nearby to store on board. There was urgent work for the blacksmith, so wood was required for his smithy in addition to the needs of the charcoal burners.[20]

The rudder of *Espérance* was found to have its iron fittings worn, so they were dismantled to allow the blacksmith to repair it. The iron tiller rod was bent and anchor chains needed attention. Within eight days these essential repairs were completed. Lieutenant Denis de Trobriand was pleased to note in the ship's log 'that the repairs were perfect' and he paid credit to 'the skill of our carpenters and blacksmith'.[21] Their forge and the *Recherche* observatory were situated on the modern Motts Beach.

On 3 February 1793, gunner Boucher was buried ashore. He died a lingering death from tuberculosis and many of his shipmates attended the service, presumably in the Cockle Creek area.[22] A cemetery there today, however, is a relic of the post-nineteenth century establishment of the abortive Ramsgate settlement. This unknown grave presumably was the first European interment in Tasmania, just as Louise Gerardin was the first European woman to visit that island.

Some animals were probably consigned to a rapid death by spearing. A male and female goat were released on the bay's southern shore by d'Entrecasteaux. 'It is to be hoped,' d'Auribeau reported, 'that for the sake of visiting seamen the two animals will be very successful and become a useful resource at this port.' Plans to release a doe and a stag deer there were thwarted when the stag died at sea.[23]

Recherche Bay

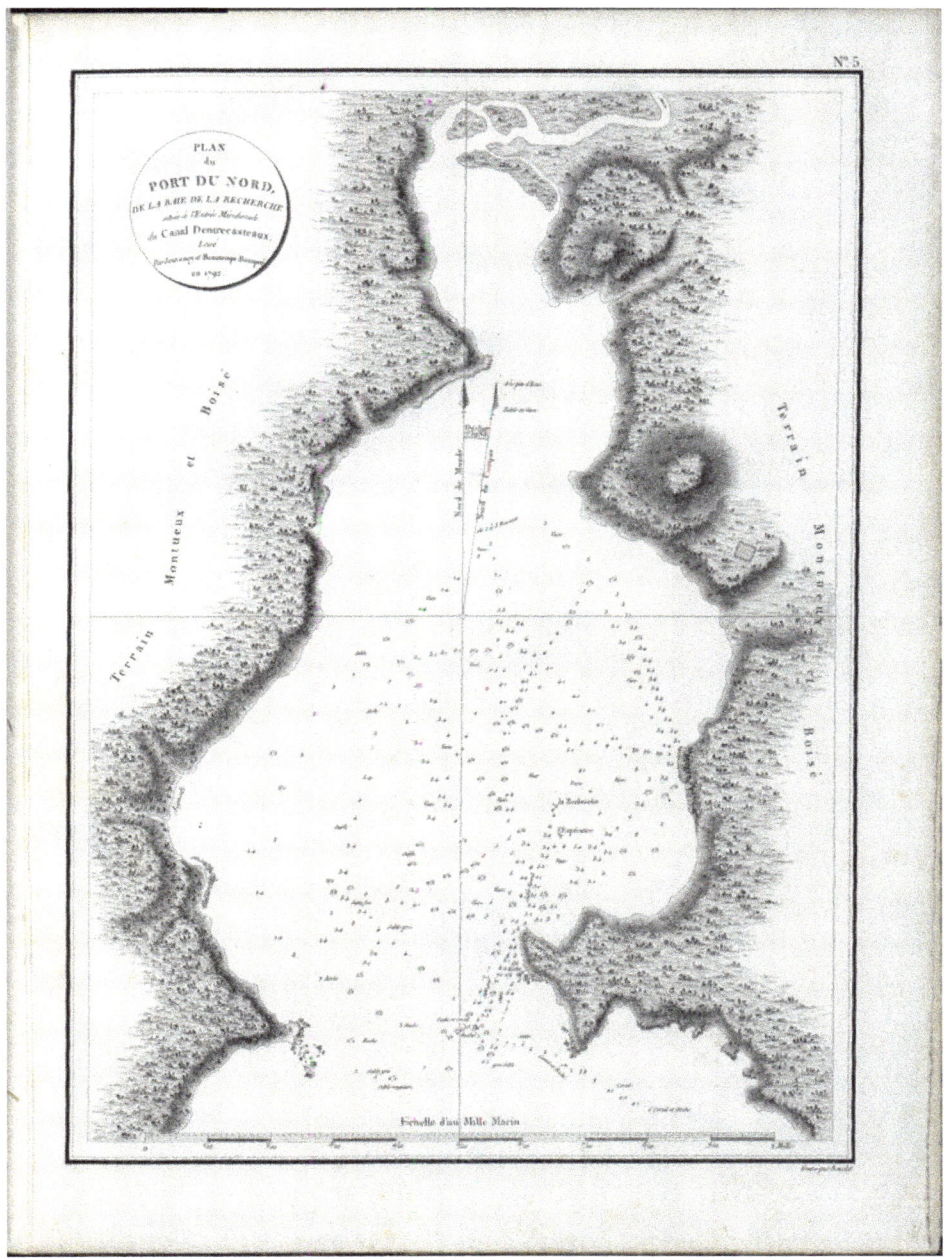

Beautemps-Beaupré's chart showing the 1792 harbour anchorage. National Library of Australia

Beautemps-Beaupré's chart of northern harbour (Pigsties Bay), indicating 1792 anchorage, Observatory Point and the garden square (jardin) middle right. Published in *Atlas du voyage de Bruny-Dentrecasteaux...*, Depot general des cartes et plans de la marine et des colonies, Paris, 1807. National Library of Australia [map ra82-s7]

Marine resources again were a prime objective for food and must have bolstered health and stamina, as they were eaten in abundance. D'Auribeau complained that sailors on *Recherche* were slack fisherman when compared with the rival crew. In addition to ample quantities of various fish species, shellfish, especially mussels and oysters, were plentiful. Oysters were particularly accessible on rocks near Observatory Point. Crayfish were another welcome resource. Some inventive sailor constructed a trap from netting 'made up of three circles and some rods' resembling a barrel open at both ends. About 100 crayfish were harvested at one place.[24] Apart from those fish eaten by the crew, there was a considerable industry in salting and drying the fish. Towards the end of their stay, Kermadec remarked, with appreciation, that 'they hung up as decorations all round the rigging'.[25]

At the conclusion to their Tasmanian experiences, when D'Entrecasteaux Channel had been surveyed, the captains reflected upon the geographic situation. Kermadec recognised the great advantages it posed as a major shipping lane, because it was sheltered. It later provided a shorter route to Hobart. Recherche Bay was suitable for ship repairs, while water and wood were readily available. He then conjectured about the future, where hillsides 'appear suitable for plantations of vines'. 'If ever this country becomes inhabited by Europeans,' he thought, 'it is possible that the strait will become the place recommended.'[26] D'Entrecasteaux felt enraptured with the advantages of the sheltered and relatively reef-free Channel and its many harbours. 'None of the expedition's navigators had ever seen such vast and safe anchorages in their travels; all the fleets of the world could be assembled there, and there would still be ample space left.'[27]

Because of the surveying by this expedition and the quality of its charting, followed shortly by Baudin's presence nine years later, British interests became alarmed that France might annex areas. It was no coincidence, therefore, that in 1803 a settlement occurred at Risdon Cove, adjacent to the future Hobart. It might be inferred that both Kermadec and d'Entrecasteaux voiced strategic aims, and that Recherche Bay could become a way-station to the French Pacific. Yet nothing in the expedition's instructions or comments in their journals suggest political objectives. It is best to conclude that these were disinterested but enthusiastic impressions intended to benefit any vessels from all nations sailing those waters.

ENDNOTES

[1] Labillardière, *Voyage in search of La Pérouse*, 1800: 19-20, 82.

[2] Horner, *Looking for La Pérouse*, 1995: 63-8; Labillardière, *Voyage in search of La Pérouse*, 1800: 89-91; Duyker and Duyker (eds and trans), *Bruny d'Entrecasteaux: voyage to Australia and the Pacific*, 2001: 26-9.

[3] Plomley and Piard-Bernier, *The General*, 1993: 329 – du Portail.

[4] Plomley and Piard-Bernier, *The General*, 1993: 330.

[5] Labillardière, *Voyage in search of La Pérouse*, 1800: 94, 32.

[6] Plomley and Piard-Bernier, *The General*, 1993: 64 – log of *Recherche*.

[7] Flinders, *A voyage to Terra Australis*, 1814, vol. 1: xcii.

[8] Duyker and Duyker (eds and trans), *Bruny d'Entrecasteaux: voyage to Australia and the Pacific*, 2001: 35-6.

[9] Plomley and Piard-Bernier, *The General*, 1993: 95

[10] Labillardière, *Voyage in search of La Pérouse*, 1800: 93, 124; Plomley and Piard-Bernier, *The General*, 1993: 71.

[11] Plomley and Piard-Bernier, *The General*, 1993: 109 – d'Auribeau, 72 – Trobriand; Labillardière, *Voyage in search of La Pérouse*, 1800: 118.

[12] County of Kent, Parish of Purves, survey by district surveyor George Innes, November 1863, number 046646.

[13] Plomley and Piard-Bernier, *The General*, 1993: 66-73 – log entries.

[14] Plomley and Piard-Bernier, *The General*, 1993: 75.

[15] Plomley and Piard-Bernier, *The General*, 1993: 332 – du Portail.

[16] Plomley and Piard-Bernier, *The General*, 1993: 68.

[17] Ibid.: 69.

[18] Plomley and Piard-Bernier, *The General*, 1993: 336-7 – du Portail.

[19] Plomley and Piard-Bernier, *The General*, 1993: 199 – d'Auribeau; Duyker and Duyker (eds and trans), *Bruny d'Entrecasteaux: voyage to Australia and the Pacific*, 2001: 138.

[20] Plomley and Piard-Bernier, *The General*, 1993: 149.

[21] Ibid.: 156.

[22] Labillardière, *Voyage in search of La Pérouse*, 1800: 293; Plomley and Piard-Bernier, *The General*, 1993: 158 – log entry; Richard, *Le Voyage de d'Entrecasteaux*, 1986: 135 – Ladroux.

[23] Plomley and Piard-Bernier, *The General*, 1993: 196-7 – d'Auribeau.

[24] Plomley and Piard-Bernier, *The General*, 1993: 197 – d'Auribeau, 165 – Pilot Raoul.

[25] Plomley and Piard-Bernier, *The General*, 1993: 117 – Kermadec.

[26] Plomley and Piard-Bernier, *The General*, 1993: 123.

[27] Duyker and Duyker (eds and trans), *Bruny d'Entrecasteaux: voyage to Australia and the Pacific*, 2001: 48.

Chapter 3: Naturalists Ashore

When the naturalists disembarked and commenced exploration it proved a welcome relief. 'It is difficult to express the sensations we felt,' Labillardière exclaimed romantically, 'at finding ourselves at length sheltered in this solitary harbour at the extremity of the globe.'[1] His English contemporary, William Wordsworth, would have been in sympathy: 'On Man, on Nature and on Human Life, Musing in Solitude.'

Although French orders were to deal humanely with indigenous peoples, at their initial landing nobody knew what reception they might receive from the unknown and unseen inhabitants. Consequently, each naturalist entered the peninsula's forest warily and well armed. They were relieved at first to meet neither foe nor friend. Soon, however, they wished for some contact, because they were intrigued by the sight of distant smokes, and the huts, fireplaces and artefacts they commonly encountered throughout their journeys. Obviously they were being watched by invisible but peaceful Tasmanians, and so it remained during their 1792 visitation. Labillardière reported somewhat ruefully: 'though a great number of men from both vessels had penetrated very far into the country, they had not met with a single inhabitant'.[2]

Riche became lost during his first foray at Recherche Bay and spent a fearful night in the forest, which he imagined was populated with 'savages'. He suffered nothing but discomfort. Riche obviously was a keen fieldworker lacking a sense of direction. During the following year, while the expedition was surveying the Recherche Archipelago, Western Australia, he again became lost and only returned to the anxious officers on the third day. By this time, d'Entrecasteaux had decided to sail, leaving behind some rations and a musket for the castaway. Labillardière challenged his decision, no doubt providing a humane defence, which included the example of James Cook who waited for a lost sailor.[3] Fortunately, an exhausted Riche returned before the final departure resulted. This foolish incident angered d'Entrecasteaux, who deplored the foolhardiness of Riche going ashore alone. To cover himself, he wrote a full account in his journal, because he had more than enough of gentlemen naturalists who did not observe prudent rules. 'The advantage of using persons employed in the navy for these kinds of expedition cannot be stressed enough,' he wrote in exasperation, 'since persons (being more aware of what is permitted in such circumstances) would not make impossible demands and would be less disposed to attribute ill-will.'[4]

In relating Riche's adventure at Recherche Bay, du Portail provided Zélie with an amusing but unsympathetic pen portrait of a typical savant, for whom he felt no affinity, in common with most of his fellow officers. Riche may have been an imprudent loner, but for du Portail he typified the 'naturalist' species.

> You have read Robinson Crusoe haven't you? You can picture him on his island with his ludicrous accoutrement, can you not! So there! It is more or less the same as the case of our naturalist! He wears a baggy duck jacket with a pocket on the front and at the back. A big portfolio is used as a game bag and stays on his loins, a mineralogist's hammer hangs below it, and a piece of card over the opposite shoulder is used to hang some forceps padded with linen, these to catch insects and butterflies. A pad covered with long pins is tied to his buttonhole and, lastly, a sword or broad bladed knife hangs at his side. To be in keeping with the umbrella, he wears a broad-brimmed leather hat to ensure some shadow for his head and some leather gaiters as a protection against all that could harm him and, of course, the usual gun is there to complete this mass of equipment.[5]

Rather than a cartoon character, du Portail describes a well-equipped fieldworker, competent to deal with any component of the natural world he stumbled upon, while his clothing and hat sensibly met variable weather conditions. Kermadec described Riche as 'a very zealous naturalist'.[6] Certainly he was burdened. However, Riche had a servant who should have shared the load of the natural world's harvest.

This servant found, however, that at Recherche Bay he served two masters. He had been ill and was treated by naval surgeon Denis Joannet, who was making his own collection of birds in rivalry with Riche. When this servant shot some birds for Riche, Joannet demanded them as his right because the man was his patient. When the servant refused and remained loyal to Riche, the doctor warned him of retribution. This came in the form of a purgative which Joannet forced upon his patient, with predictable dire consequences. Labillardière, who recorded this ridiculous episode, reflected that 'melancholy experience' showed that Joannet must be obeyed.[7] In this situation Riche's servant's assistance was problematic.

Although the naturalists made exciting and important discoveries, they encountered indifference or hostility from the naval personnel. The fact that most naturalists were republicans (and Labillardière accorded them the title of 'citizen' in his book) ensured tensions and rivalries with the royalist officers. Some officers seemed totally indifferent to scientific discoveries, of whom d'Auribeau was a representative. 'The naturalists,' he wrote, 'have made their investigations with zeal … and it seems to me they have made an extensive collection. I do not doubt they have found objects which are both new and extremely unusual.'[8] He neither questioned what they had found, or what it implied for learning.

It was their freedom from naval regulations and their egalitarian civilian attitudes that concerned d'Entrecasteaux, who found their requirements unreasonable, as his journal entry concerning the Riche incident made clear. The naturalists did have a case, however, because they were subjected to petty discrimination by some officers. Some examples follow.

When naturalists went ashore they received a ration of ship's biscuit, cheese, brandy and sometimes salted bacon. Fresh fruit or other provisions were not allowed, following a decision by the officers which was adhered to strictly. Upon returning to the shore from excursions, naturalists encountered delays with boats coming to pick them up, while officers took precedence when space was limited.[9]

It was the restricted rations when a party stayed on shore overnight which rankled most with the savants. It should be remembered that they knew nothing about the availability of 'bush tucker' and, except for Labillardière, were not tempted to experiment. Sometimes they found fish or shellfish, even shooting two birds on one occasion. Louis Ventenat was not satisfied with the issue of 'some cheese, some biscuit filled with grubs and a little bit of bad wine'.[10] Labillardière's version added salty bacon to the ration, but he complained that they were entitled to fresh provisions.[11] Eating one of these unpalatable meals one night in the forest, he remarked ruefully, that 'such a supper as this certainly required a good appetite'.

Equally grievous was d'Entrecasteaux's failure to supply Labillardière with a servant who could assist him in preparing and storing botanical specimens. This proved a time-consuming task aboard, requiring one or two days, so losing botanical time ashore. Judging from his book, he spent almost eight days, one quarter of their stay, arranging his collection. In his frustration, he claimed that 'he had every right to expect' such aid.[12] That his hundreds of specimens survive today is testimony to the care he took in their drying and packing, despite his impatience to be ashore.

Labillardière was a senior scientist with a stubborn, rumbustious, bourgeois character, so he tried the patience of the well-known Admiral. He stirred a confrontation during their first week at Recherche Bay when he and Ventenat returned weary and hungry to the beach at nightfall. They waited two hours for a boat, so Labillardière vented his displeasure on the dinghy's coxwain. His complaints were conveyed to d'Entrecasteaux.

The commander, according to Ventenat, 'got into a sudden temper and in his cabin treated the naturalist in a manner so indecent that the master of a school would have blushed at it, exclaiming in a loud voice "that one was in no way allowed to disturb the supper of the crew" … He brushed aside our replies, saying that the supreme power with which he had been invested permitted him to do ... just as he wished'.[13]

Another cause of disagreement concerned Labillardière's use of the great cabin. His tiny cabin soon became overcrowded with specimens as botanical collecting boomed. He required space to dry and press all plants. Consequently he shifted his operations into the great cabin, an area used by all officers. Objections from d'Auribeau were soon forthcoming, as he ordered the plant presses out. Upon their removal they were deposited in an area exposed to rain. The space underneath the large table also was a convenient place to store two boxes containing completed specimens, pressed between large sheets of paper. Spare and precious paper, of which 22 reams had been brought aboard after much trouble in locating sheets large enough, also was stored in these boxes. They were unceremoniously removed. An angry and stubborn Labillardière appealed to d'Entrecasteaux, who reasonably ruled that the botanists might continue to use the cabin facilities. Presumably this agitation further strained relations between officers and naturalists.[14]

Ventenat, a fellow botanist, felt equally put upon by these inconveniences and by the theft of some of the valuable paper. In accounting for these actions, he observed that d'Entrecasteaux 'is an honest man and well disposed, of a pleasing appearance, intrepid, but of too easygoing a character, even too good: the serious illness of his second-in-command [d'Auribeau] gives him cause for concern and he can refuse him nothing. As for the rest he fears to attract the odium of the senior officers'.[15]

Regardless of tensions — political, social and intellectual — as discussed later, this expedition at Recherche Bay achieved eminence in the scientific fields of botany, geomagnetism, surveying and cartography, anthropology and race relations. It endowed this harbour and precinct with international significance.

Unfortunately, these French achievements do not accord with Australian national sentiment, as promulgated by the Howard government, which accords iconic status to British navigators. Tasmanian waters, in particular, were sailed by heroes Cook, Bligh, Flinders and Bass. Had Recherche Bay been discovered and explored by any of those popular captains, the future of the area might have been more secure. Even today, a review of the National Museum of Australia in Canberra recommended that the Captain Cook saga should be a priority, although a visitor might expect such a promotion to be displayed at the National Maritime Museum in Sydney.

ENDNOTES

[1] Labillardière, *Voyage in search of La Pérouse*. 1800: 94. Wordsworth, *The Excursion*, preface.

[2] Labillardière, *Voyage in search of La Pérouse*. 1800: 104.

[3] Labillardière, *Voyage in search of La Pérouse*, 1800: 266-73; Horner, *Looking for La Pérouse*, 1995: 120.

[4] Duyker and Duyker (eds and trans), *Bruny d'Entrecasteaux: voyage to Australia and the Pacific*, 2001: 127.

[5] Plomley and Piard-Bernier, *The General*, 1993: 331 – du Portail.

[6] Plomley and Piard-Bernier, *The General*, 1993: 118 – Kermadec.

[7] Labillardière, *Voyage in search of La Pérouse*, 1800: 97-8

[8] Plomley and Piard-Bernier, *The General*, 1993: 111 – d'Auribeau.

[9] Labillardière, *Voyage in search of La Pérouse*, 1800: 106, 126, 98.

[10] Plomley and Piard-Bernier, *The General*, 1993: 352 – Ventenat.

[11] Labillardière, *Voyage in search of La Pérouse*, 1800: 104.

[12] Duyker, *Citizen Labillardière*, 2003: 103.

[13] Labillardière, *Voyage in search of La Pérouse*. 1800: 98; Plomley and Piard-Bernier, *The General*, 1993: 354 – Ventenat.

[14] Labillardière, *Voyage in search of La Pérouse*, 1800: 22, 109; Plomley and Piard-Bernier, *The General*, 1993: 352-3 – Ventenat.

[15] Plomley and Piard-Bernier, *The General*, 1993: 353.

Chapter 4: Botanising

During the eighteenth century, the Linnaean classification of flora enabled botany to be systematised and provided with a global reference. Linnaean taxonomy and nomenclature expedited the reduction of plants to specimens, numbers and names. Once a specimen was so identified, it represented that plant type no matter where it was found. In the heart of Paris, the *Jardin du Roi* was a central powerhouse for organising research which could benefit both science and the nation. Closely allied with the navy, its botanists encouraged the collection of plants from overseas.

Global botany and the economic utilisation of newly found plants became national goals. By the time of the d'Entrecasteaux expedition there existed some 1,600 botanical gardens in Europe. They connected scientific discovery and identification with experimentation in transferred plants and acclimatisation. The best known example in the British Empire of transplanting in imperial economic interests is William Bligh's breadfruit laden HMS *Bounty*.[1] Gardener Delahaye also was to successfully transfer breadfruit from the Pacific to Ile de France. As Schiebinger and Swan wrote recently in *Colonial Botany*: 'The story of colonial botany is as much a story of transplanting nature as it is one of transferring knowledge.'[2]

When Labillardière stepped ashore in Tasmania, he was a senior French botanist trained in the Linnaean tradition, having studied at the *Jardin du Roi*. He was a dedicated scientist, seeking to enlarge knowledge of global flora, but equally, he was concerned to find plants that had economic or commercial potential. Eyewitness to scurvy's scourge, it is hardly surprising that he was alert to edible plants that could serve as food at sea. He accumulated one of the largest herbarium collections of that era.

Labillardière's experience and reputation made him the foremost botanist until that time to enter an Australian forest. Imbued with Rousseauesque sentiments concerning nature and man, he immediately was stimulated by the vista of cool temperate rainforest. 'The eye is astonished,' he enthused, 'in contemplating the prodigious size of these trees ... whose tufted summits were crowned with an ever verdant foliage: others, loosened by age from their roots, were supported by neighbouring trees, whilst, as they gradually decayed, they were incorporated ... with the parent-earth ... a striking picture of the operations of nature, who, left to herself, never destroys but that she may again create.'[3]

D'Entrecasteaux was equally enlivened by the romantic landscape: 'It will be difficult,' he exclaimed, 'to describe my feelings at the sight of this solitary harbour at the extremities of the world, so perfectly enclosed that one feels separated from the rest of the universe. Everything is influenced by the wilderness of the rugged landscape. With each step, one encounters the beauties of unspoilt nature.'[4]

Most of their botanising task took place during 1792 on, or north of, the north-eastern peninsula opposite their anchorage. To this were added the 1793 collections on the harbour's western and southern rim, but in this discussion both visits are linked. The dense rainforest seen by the French was depleted following the establishment in 1884 of the Leprena sawmill. Fortunately, harvesting methods of that era did not involve total devastation. There are still impressive stands which recall the French wonderment, while on the peninsula timber regrowth is sufficient to suggest that green forested vision of two centuries ago. From the heritage viewpoint comes another consideration. Should modern invasive technological timber harvesting take place, the type localities of the many plant species collected here will be ravaged, apart from the destruction of archaeological evidence.

During Labillardière's first afternoon ashore on the peninsula where so much of his research took place, he reported that he gathered several eucalypt species. By the time that they sailed, during the 33 days available for land-based exploration (minus about eight days lost preparing specimens aboard), Louis Ventenat claimed that they had collected some 5,000 specimens (presumably including leaves, flowers, fruit and seeds). According to Ventenat, these represented up to 500 species and 30 genera, probably including the 1793 collections.[5] As Edward Duyker points out, labelling or memory confusion mixed into this total some specimens collected in Western Australia. Making allowances for generous counting by Ventenat and for labelling errors, the botanists still made a very impressive collection during their periods on shore. Their Tasmanian floral collections are admirably presented in *The General*.[6]

When the botanists explored, they took with them the only artist on the voyage. Piron is little known, but Labillardière fortunately mentions him in passing. On one occasion he made 'several drawings of the landscape,' and on another he instructed Piron to draw specimens that they had collected.[7] Unfortunately, most of Piron's invaluable drawings were lost and only 15 engraved plates based upon his sketches were included in Labillardière's publications.[8] Recent research by Edward Duyker has established that his given name was Jean and that he was a Belgian who probably never returned to Europe.[9]

Through his strenuous activities Labillardière established one of the largest herbariums of those times, while he published the first major general description of Australian flora. His two-volume *Novae Hollandiae Plantarum Specimen*, which was published between 1804 and 1807, contained 265 copperplate engravings of Australian species. British reports on limited subjects preceded this publication, but France has the honour of precedence for the first major study. It represented an exceptional exercise in scientific analysis, description and illustration. Recherche Bay was endowed with international significance through its contribution to the identification of Australian flora and its association with a distinguished European botanist.

Type specimen of *Eucalyptus globulus (blue gum)*. National Library of Australia

The type specimen of *Eucalyptus globulus* (blue gum) published by Labillardière in 1800. Engraving in *Atlas pour servir a la relation du voyage a la recherché de la Perouse*, Paris: Chez Dabo, 1817. Plate 13. National Library of Australia [nla.pic-an20974042]

To judge from Labillardière's own account, 6 May 1792 was a day of considerable satisfaction, for this was his most noteworthy discovery, when he had a blue gum felled to collect flowers. He named, described and illustrated *Eucalyptus globulus* in his 1800 publication. Its great height proved a source of wonderment, but satisfaction also, for its tall straight trunk appeared to hold potential for ship building. To his delight, the carpenters found blue gum timbers the most suitable for providing planks to raise the gunwales on the oared boats.[10]

Labillardière could hardly have anticipated the great commercial advantages of his discovery: that it was introduced rapidly around the world as a cultivar, becoming the species by which the genus *Eucalyptus* became internationally known; that by 1905 four million feet of its timber would be supplied to the British Admiralty for wharf piles; that today more than 1.3 million hectares of *E. globulus* are planted outside Australia and 0.4 million hectares of plantation within Australia; or that Tasmania would adopt it as its State floral emblem.[11]

In addition to blue gum, Labillardière collected six of the 29 eucalypt species now known to be native to Tasmania. These included *Eucalyptus cordata* (Tasmanian silver gum), *E. ovata* (swamp gum), *E. viminalis* (ribbon gum) and *E. amygdalina* (black peppermint). He also collected *E. pulchella* (white peppermint), but this was not described until after his death.[12] He also attributed another plant to *Eucalyptus resinifera* (red mahogany), which he incorrectly believed had been described by John White at Sydney (actually J. E. Smith described it for White). Labillardière was wrong, because this species does not grow in Tasmania. However, as he observed that *E. globulus* closely resembled *E. resinifera*, his confusion seems understandable.[13]

Edward Duyker, in his detailed biography of *Citizen Labillardière*, discussed the many other plants collected and named by his hero. Some plants had been found previously, so they lacked priority, or were incorrectly identified; these were in the minority.[14] Some notable discoveries included the evergreen native cherry, whose nut resembled the cashew. Labillardière recognised it as a new genus, naming it *Exocarpus cupressiformis*.[15] Other botanical finds included four species of heath (*Epacris*), including *Epacris impressa*. The latter became Victoria's floral emblem, so both Victoria and Tasmania chose floral emblems collected and named by Labillardière, surely a special association between person and place of collection. Further plants credited to him included four orchid species, flag iris (*Diplarrena moraea*), Christmas bells (*Blandfordia punicea*) and the sedge, *Gahnia*.

One plant which provided significant but temporary 'bush tucker' was *Apium prostratum*, 'sea celery'. Labillardière tasted it and found it good to eat, so quantities were gathered and taken aboard as welcome fresh vegetable 'greens'. On a later excursion some species of plantago (*Plantago muelleri*?) were tried and eaten with 'relish'.[16] Possibly because the botanists only met Aboriginal people at the end of their Recherche Bay visit, they were unable to profit from their knowledge of plant foods. Reference was made to the Aboriginal people eating plants but nobody seems to have followed this up by tasting such food items.[17] Some food sources such as seaweed and roots of rushes may have seemed too unattractive, even though they saw them cooked and eaten on several occasions.

Labillardière, Ventenat and Delahaye merit credit for the discomfort that they accepted on their land excursions. The first deterrent was the inconvenience and hunger from the meagre and monotonous rations provided by their ships. Significantly, this restricted the time they could be absent from shipboard meals. Occasionally they shot birds and collected shellfish, but the bush supplied only a small proportion of their diet. Their camping equipment was minimal. Despite the cold and frequent rain, their only protection was the brush shelters they erected, while sleeping on beds of fern. They huddled near large fires because generally the weather during autumn 1792 proved 'very sharp'; even during their summertime visit in 1793, the cold proved 'very piercing'.[18]

Then there were the insects in this unfamiliar land. A bad night resulted from 'the fury of the mosquitoes,' while Ventenat was assaulted by ferocious ants when he slipped upon a huge fallen trunk which proved rotten. Not only did the fall cut his lips and tongue, but he lost a tooth, while the ants 'swarmed over me in their thousands'. '[W]e were plagued by very large flies,' complained D'Entrecasteaux. 'In general the flies are much more amazing ... than in our climates.' Perhaps these were March flies, as their 'buzzing is very loud and troublesome'.[19]

During 1793 the botanists adventured into the wilderness. On one occasion they followed what probably was an Aboriginal track from Cockle Creek to South Cape Bay. Passing a night there, Delahaye complained that 'we had never previously felt so cold'.[20] The snow covered peak of Mt La Pérouse beckoned, for in the clear air it seemed deceptively close, while nearer ranges were concealed by the vegetation. On 31 January 1793, an expedition of 11 men set out for the mountains with food for four days. To judge from Labillardière's account they spent a gruelling time penetrating the forest, walking above ground upon wet and rotten fallen vegetation. They ascended a hill with great exertion, possibly Mt Leillateah, and were daunted by the forested distance remaining to their mountainous objective. They turned back, because rations would not last the time required, as 'these forests ... afforded nothing' to eat, which added prudence to the adverse wet and cold conditions.[21]

Half the party headed towards the southern coast, while the remainder returned to base. On their south-eastern journey towards South Cape Bay, they noticed a thin seam of coal, the first record made of coal in Tasmania.[22] They slept that night in the brush shelter that they had constructed on their recent visit. They continued collecting plant specimens with some difficulty because the sailors carrying their specimen boxes could not get through the rocks and forest blocking access. 'We were obliged to collect plants in our handkerchiefs,' Delahaye remarked in irritation. Amongst their finds were two new lobelia species and, floating on two large pools, they collected the bladderwort *Utricularia dichotoma*. They arrived back on board to learn that gunner Boucher had died. Because their food supply had been inadequate, Delahaye reported that they returned with a 'ferocious appetite'.[23]

The Garden

During this exploration era it became a common practice for visiting vessels in newly discovered lands to plant European flora and release domestic animals. It was hoped that the animals would breed and that the plants would spread, thereby providing sustenance for future crews or castaways. A secondary expectation was that the animals and plants would prove useful to Aboriginal inhabitants and so induce them to become 'civilised'. 'Maybe one day,' reflected La Motte du Portail, 'the natives will give thanks to the French for having provided them with a substantial source of food.'[24]

William Bligh planted fruit trees at Adventure Bay, Bruny Island, during his HMS *Bounty* visit in 1788 and his HMS *Providence* stopover in 1792. When d'Entrecasteaux anchored there a few months later, Delahaye found that one of the seven trees planted that year had died, and he pruned the rest. An apple tree, presumably planted during 1788, was almost two metres high, but was in a 'very bad state'. He pruned it, but was unable to find any other planting.

It is an agreeable conceit to credit Bligh as the father of Tasmania's apple industry, with input from France, though there is no evidence that his trees prospered. Certainly, republican Labillardière gave Bligh no praise, reporting the following undemocratic notice nailed to a tree:

> Near this tree Captain William Bligh planted seven fruit trees, 1792. Messrs. S. and W. Botanists.[25]

Labillardière remarked in disgust that this and similar inscriptions 'all displayed the same marks of deference which the English botanists paid the commander of their ship, by putting only the initial letters of their own names, and expressing that the Captain himself had sowed and planted ... I am much inclined to doubt, whether Bligh was very sensible to the honour.'

Delahaye commenced gardening immediately upon their arrival in 1792, planting cress, which germinated after three days, presumably a crop intended for crew meals. According to the *Recherche* Log, he and two men were instructed to prepare a garden on 10 May. As the site of this garden is disputed today — hardly surprising since no archaeological investigation has been attempted at the time of writing — it is important to present the existing evidence.

Significantly, the log entry reports that 'the place they select will be shown on the chart of the bay,'[26] and on the meticulous map prepared by Beautemps-Beaupré the garden was 1.3 kilometres NNE of Bennetts Point and 70 metres in from Coal Pit Bight.

It is appropriate to begin with Delahaye's own account, in which he makes clear that this was not the only scene of horticultural activities.

> two men and myself tilled with great difficulty, a piece of land measuring 28 feet square. I sowed plants suitable for the season, which are celery, chervil, chicory, cabbages, grey romaine lettuce, different kinds of turnip, white onion, radishes, sorrel, peas, black salsify and potatoes. I had large quantities sewn everywhere in the woods, in the more open spaces and where the soil was more friable. It was not possible to sow any more in the soil which is very difficult to cultivate, and in the season which did not allow it. I sowed mixed seeds everywhere thrown at random, where I believed they could succeed.[27]

Historians are indebted to Maryse Duyker for this recent translation from Delahaye's difficult manuscript in archaic regional dialect and almost indecipherable writing. It adds considerably to our knowledge of the number and variety of species of seeds planted and to other plantings. From Labillardière we learn that the garden measured nine metres by seven metres, that it was divided into four sections and that he judged the soil as unsuitable because it consisted largely of clay,[28] so the area in Delahaye's note quoted above may be in error. It is important to observe that Delahaye sowed seeds elsewhere, and du Portail in 1793 also cleared 'a small square of garden'. Such sites may yet be discovered.[29] One such garden was prepared somewhere in the Cockle Creek area while Labillardière and Delahaye were absent attempting mountaineering. Labillardière had hoped to plant in fertile soil, but 'I saw with regret that a very dry and very sandy spot, pretty near the head of the bay, had been dug up and sown'.[30]

Upon the expedition's return in 1793, Delahaye and Labillardière landed on the peninsula where they had collected the previous year. On 6 February they collected further plants, intending to revisit the garden site. The following morning they set out early each with a pruning-knife and handkerchief to carry specimens. It was then that they first made contact with Aboriginal people. Despite early tension, the meeting went well, but the garden was visited in company with a number of men. Perhaps these preoccupations resulted in a cursory inspection, because Delahaye simply recorded: 'All the seeds had nearly sprouted, but remained with their first leaves'; it was 'in a very poor state'.[31] He blamed the drought.

'The axe had never sounded'

The 'garden' in 2003, outlined by rocks. John Mulvaney

The 'garden' in 2003 outlined by rocks, approx. 9 x 7m. John Mulvaney

D'Entrecasteaux was interested in the fate of garden and, to judge from his journal, Delahaye returned for another inspection: 'M. La Haye inspected it with more care than on the first occasion; he found a few chicory plants, cabbages, sorrel, radishes, cress and a few potatoes had grown, but had only produced the first two seminal leaves.' Delahaye now blamed the lack of success on 'the seeds having been sown in too advanced a season'.[32] Labillardière blamed the lack of water and expressed surprise that at least some cress had not been planted closer to a nearby stream.[33]

Whatever the explanation for the garden's failure, apart from Bligh's incipient orchard, this was the first attempt to cultivate vegetables in Tasmania. As it is well documented and located on a chart, it is important to establish the credentials of the feature discovered early in 2003. It should be noted that the size of the garden on Beautemps-Beaupré's chart is much larger in area. Possibly it was surveyed from the sea, with its location on the map only indicative. With stones carefully laid to define an area some nine by seven metres, it suggests that this historic garden has been identified over two centuries since it was dug and planted. As Tasmania's first garden (like Bligh's token orchard) it holds an honourable place in the history of gardening in Australia. As Tasmania's Botany Bay, Recherche Bay is the type site for many Australian plants.

ENDNOTES

[1] Schiebinger and Swan, *Colonial botany*, 2005: 5-17.
[2] Ibid.: 17.
[3] Labillardière, *Voyage in search of La Pérouse*, 1800: 96.
[4] Duyker and Duyker (eds and trans) *Bruny d'Entrecasteaux: voyage to Australia and the Pacific*, 2001: 32.
[5] Plomley and Piard-Bernier, *The General*, 1993: 356 – Ventenot.
[6] Duyker, *Citizen Labillardière*, 2003: 98; Plomley and Piard-Bernier, *The General*, 1993: 233-41.
[7] Labillardière, *Voyage in search of La Pérouse*, 1800: 101, 113.
[8] Duyker, *Citizen Labillardière*, 2003: 231.
[9] Duyker, *National Library of Australia News* March (2006): 7-10.
[10] Labillardière, *Voyage in search of La Pérouse*, 1800: 111-112, 118.
[11] Potts and Reid, *Papers and Proceedings Royal Society of Tasmania* 137 (2003): 25.
[12] Ibid.: 21.
[13] Labillardière, *Voyage in search of La Pérouse*, 1800: 111; Duyker, *Citizen Labillardière*, 2003: 99.
[14] Duyker, *Citizen Labillardière*, 2003: 98-110, 141-6.
[15] Labillardière, *Voyage in search of La Pérouse*, 1800: 113.
[16] Ibid.: 105, 287.
[17] Duyker, *Citizen Labillardière*, 2003: 143.
[18] Labillardière, *Voyage in search of La Pérouse*, 1800: 103, 286.
[19] Labillardière, *Voyage in search of La Pérouse*, 1800: 292 – mosquitoes; Plomley and Piard-Bernier, *The General*, 1993: 350 – ants; Duyker and Duyker (eds and trans), *Bruny d'Entrecasteaux: voyage to Australia and the Pacific*, 2001: 140 – flies.
[20] Duyker and Duyker, *Explorations* 37 (2004): 37.
[21] Labillardière, *Voyage in search of La Pérouse*, 1800: 290.
[22] Ibid.: 291.

[23] Duyker and Duyker, *Explorations* 37 (2004): 39; Labillardière, *Voyage in search of La Pérouse*, 1800: 292-3.
[24] Plomley and Piard-Bernier, *The General*, 1993: 119.
[25] Duyker and Duyker, *Explorations* 37 (2004): 42; Labillardière, *Voyage in search of La Pérouse*, 1800: 324; Mulvaney, *Encounters in place*, 1989: 36-7.
[26] Plomley and Piard-Bernier, *The General*, 1993: 119.
[27] Duyker and Duyker, *Explorations* 37 (2004): 36.
[28] Labillardière, *Voyage in search of La Pérouse*, 1800: 118.
[29] Plomley and Piard-Bernier, *The General*, 1993: 299 – du Portail's garden.
[30] Labillardière, *Voyage in search of La Pérouse*, 1800: 293.
[31] Duyker and Duyker, *Explorations* 37 (2004): 41.
[32] Duyker and Duyker (eds and trans), *Bruny d'Entrecasteaux: voyage to Australia and the Pacific*, 2001: 141-2.
[33] Labillardière, *Voyage in search of La Pérouse*, 1800: 302.

Chapter 5: Measuring and Charting

The dominant British orientation in the teaching of Australian history and science, together with the iconic status of James Cook and Matthew Flinders, has hampered the recognition of foreign contributions, none moreso than that of the d'Entrecasteaux expedition. This neglect was assisted by the deaths en route of the commander and prominent officers, the contemporary Napoleonic wars and the delayed publication of the journal of d'Entrecasteaux compiled and edited by Rossel in 1808, but never translated into English until 2001. Contrast this with Labillardière, whose account was twice published in English translation during 1800.

The recent Australian-based publications on the expedition by Frank Horner (1995) and Edward Duyker (2001, 2003), following upon Hélène Richard's (1986) Paris-based study, have resurrected interest in this significant maritime episode. Following discussion of the expedition's botanical research, it is time to consider the physical sciences.

The expedition left Brest equipped with state-of-the-art navigation and geomagnetic equipment.[1] Items included for each ship were a telescope to observe eclipses of Jupiter's moons and an azimuth compass, a minutely divided mariner's compass fitted with vertical sights, used for taking the magnetic azimuth of a heavenly body. A navigational marine chronometer, only perfected during the later eighteenth century, was the essential tool for Rossel to determine longitude at sea.

At this period (and until 1911) French time was based on the Paris meridian, not Greenwich, so it was 2° 20′ east of Greenwich. To ascertain the local meridian of longitude a chronometer reading was taken at local noon, as indicated by the sun being at its highest point in the sky, north or south. Then each hour by which this determination of local noon differed from Paris noon (as kept by the chronometer) indicated a longitude difference from Paris of 15°.

The scientific instruments included an inclination compass by the hydrographer (then termed geographer) Jean-Claude Borda (1733–99). This instrument was like a regular compass but mounted in a vertical plane, allowing the pivotal magnetic needle to dip and so measure the magnetic 'dip' (or 'inclination'). Measurements of magnetic dip were important for charting Earth's magnetic field.

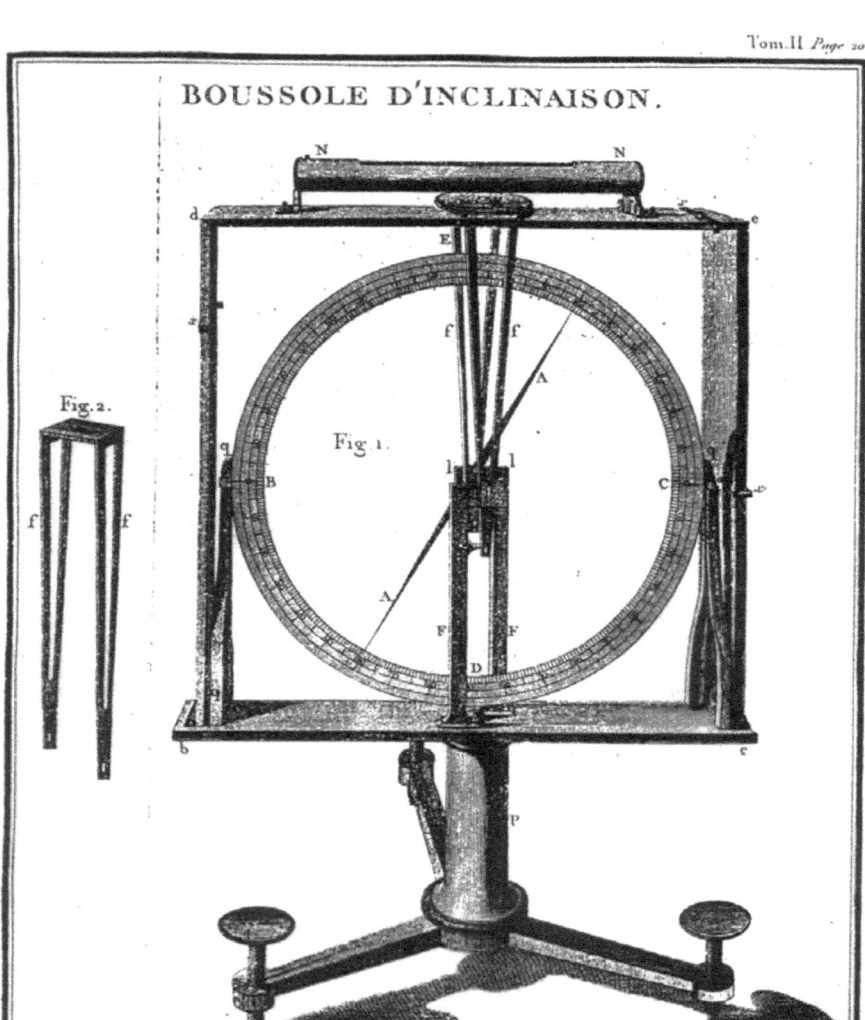

The dip needle used by Rossel. D'Entrecasteaux journal, 1808

The dip needle instrument used by Rossel to measure magnetic intensity. Illustrated by Rossel, D'Entrecasteux journal, 1808

The dip needle also could be used for the more advanced and, at the time, new purpose of measuring the intensity of the magnetic field. For this latter purpose the dip needle was deflected from its steady position, and the period of its oscillation or 'time of vibration' measured. This period of oscillation is less in a stronger magnetic field. It is relevant that timing the oscillating dip needle in this manner was greatly facilitated by having the chronometer for reference.

Measuring and Charting

Importantly for the quality of this expedition's navigation and charting, the ships were supplied with other adaptations by Borda. One instrument was an astronomical reflecting or repeating circle, an instrument for measuring angles, in which accuracy was obtained by repeated measurements of horizontal angles on a graduated circle. Its value was referred to in ship's log entries, as on *Espérance*, 16 May 1792, in fixing the precise location of Observatory Point: 'The large number of observations of meridian elevations of the sun and stars taken with the astronomical circle of Ms Borda have given 43° 32´ 23˝ south latitude.'[2] Each vessel also carried reflective circles, another Borda design, which permitted two stars to be sighted simultaneously through two telescopic sights, one mounted above, the other below the graduated circle, without needing to zero the instrument. It is worth noting that this expedition was equipped for survey and charting needs with alternative equipment to those expeditions led by Captain Cook, which relied upon sextants.

Upon their arrival in Recherche Bay, the first requirement was to erect a tent to house astronomical instruments. It was pitched behind the beach at Observatory (now Bennetts) Point. It was vital to take land-based astronomical readings in order to determine the accurate latitude and longitude, employing the chronometer.

de Borda's 'cercle répétiteur' (left) and 'cercle de reflexion' (right). Musée National de la Marine, Paris

Left: 'Cercle répétiteur' [Cercle hydrographique] developed by Jean-Charles de Borda, called the 'repeating circle' by British mariners. Musée national de la Marine, Paris [PH 42170 No. inv. : 11 NA 60 D]
Right: De Borda's 'cercle de réflexion', Anonymous, 1837. Musée national de la Marine, Paris [PH 170643 No. inv. 11 NA 22]

By 26 April 1792, the tent was erected and the instruments installed. A reason for haste was to observe the eclipse of one of Jupiter's moons, presumably upon that night. Rossel underestimated the time required to install and check the instruments, with the result that they were not ready for Jupiter when the time arrived. It all proved too stressful for young and enthusiastic ensign Achard de Bonvouloir, who had made involved mathematical calculations in advance of the actual passage. Labillardière cruelly reported that Bonvouloir became 'so affected by the disappointment that he wept like a child'. A year later and aboard ship, Bonvouloir and Labillardière had a verbal tiff during which Bonvouloir showed his emotional nature by hurling two bottles at his adversary. He was hauled away before he could take any further action.[3]

D'Entrecasteaux proved less affected by the failure to observe Jupiter, reporting that weather conditions prevented observation of four occurrences when stars were concealed ('occultation'). A number of other observations were successful, however, providing data which indicated that the ship's chronometers were accurate. This 'assured us of the reliance of these two methods in fixing the position of the places we were approaching'.[4] An observatory was set up again during their 1793 visit, when the longitude was possibly determined with greater precision. Making allowances for the Paris meridian, their resolution of latitude and longitude accords well with modern determinations. In 1792 their readings were 43° 32′ S latitude and 146° 57′ E longitude; the position of Observatory Point is actually 43° 32′ 41″ S and 146° 54′ 15″ E. All these observations and calculations were standard procedures, comparable to those carried out at the observatory established by Lieutenant William Dawes in 1788 at Sydney. On his third voyage, James Cook used portable tent observatories, with a large astronomical regulator clock standing inside.[5] Although not strictly research, provision of precise latitude and longitude, whether on land or sea, was a charting requirement.

Rossel was responsible for an innovative study, which resulted in the first global magnetic intensity survey, and which showed that intensity strengthened away from the equator. Measurements taken at Observatory Point in 1792 and at an observatory on Rocky Bay in 1793 provided crucial data for a global set of six magnetic intensity measurements taken both north and south of the equator and in equatorial latitudes.[6]

According to F. E. M. (Ted) Lilley, the procedure which Rossel followed was new and employed the Borda vertically mounted 'inclination' compass. As well as measuring the steady angle of dip, Rossel timed how long an oscillation of the dip needle took, when it was deflected from its steady position. In Recherche Bay the oscillation times of less than two seconds (see Table 1) were measured accurately by a technique involving a long series of oscillations lasting some three minutes. Taking the same dip needle to different parts of the globe was important, at that stage of the development of science, to obtain magnetic intensity measurements that were correct relative to each other. In modern technical terms the relationship is that magnetic intensity is inversely proportional to the square of the period of oscillation.[7]

Rossel presented his results as follows:

> By comparing the experimental results obtained during the expedition with each other it is evident that the oscillations of the needle were more rapid at Paris and Van Diemen's Land than at Surabaya in the isle of Java and at Amboyna; and therefore the magnetic force is greater near the poles than at the equator.[8]

Table 1 summarises his results:

Table 1 Rossel's magnetic intensity measurements

Station	Date	Latitude	E Longitude	Magnetic Dip	Time of vibration (sec.)
Brest	September 20, 1791	48° 24′ N	355° 34′	71° 30′ N	2.02
Teneriffe	October 21, 1791	28° 28′ N	343° 42′	62° 25′ N	2.081
Van Diemen's Land	May 11, 1792	43° 32′ S	146° 57′	70° 50′ S	1.869
Amboyna	October 9, 1792	3° 42′ S	128° 08′	20° 37′ S	2.403
Van Diemen's Land	February 7, 1793	43° 34′ S	146° 57′	72° 22′ S	1.850
Surabaya	May 9, 1794	7° 14′ S	112° 42′	25° 20′ S	2.429

Lilley, from whose articles all the above information is drawn, took a lead in urging the commemoration of the bicentenary of this internationally significant episode in the global history of geomagnetism. As a consequence of his and Alan Day's efforts, this was achieved. On 11 May 1992, precisely 200 years since the first experiment at Recherche Bay, a party of 21, representing the Specialist Group on Solid-Earth Geophysics of the Geological Society of Australia, visited Observatory Point, oscillated a dip needle and fixed a plaque to an adjacent dolerite outcrop. The French, who had nailed an inscription to a tree near Coal Pit Bight in 1792, would have considered this action an appropriate one. That senior scientists so gathered in 1992 provided independent testimony to the significance of this place over a decade before other heritage considerations became controversial.[9]

Rossel and his assistant Bonvouloir teamed with Beautemps-Beaupré, the principal marine surveyor, and Miroir-Jouvency to assist the production of a series of charts of exceptionally accurate detail and attractive format. These maps represented a significant and lasting result of the expedition.

In 1807 Beautemps-Beaupré published a fascinating folio-sized atlas of 39 large maps made during the course of the expedition.[10] Eight of these were surveyed while the ships were moored in Recherche Bay, or immediately following their departure. Most significant was their discovery and charting of D'Entrecasteaux Channel, six years before Flinders and Bass established the existence of Bass Strait. In ignorance of knowledge of Bass Strait, d'Entrecasteaux assumed that this newly charted channel, which he made sure that his hydrographers surveyed throughout, would become the major shipping lane for all eastern Australia-bound craft. Bass Strait was soon to offer a shorter and speedier alternative.

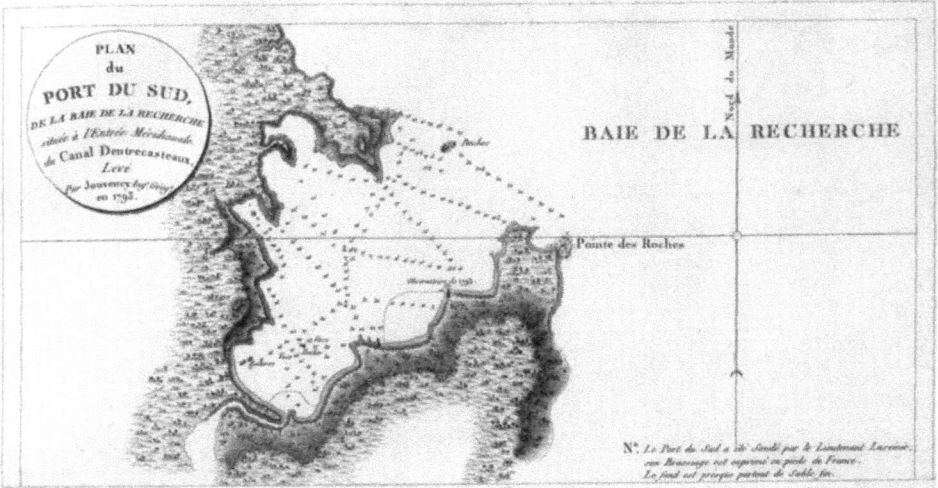

Beautemps-Beaupré's chart of Rocky Bay, southern Recherche Bay. National Library of Australia

Beautemps-Beaupré's chart of Rocky Bay, the 1793 anchorage; Cockle Creek at bottom. Published in *Atlas du voyage de Bruny-Dentrecasteaux ...*, Depot general des cartes et plans de la marine et des colonies, Paris, 1807. National Library of Australia [map ra82-s8].

Kermadec agreed with his commander, again in ignorance of Bass Strait. The Channel, he wrote, 'is formed by a series of huge bays which offer to the astounded view of the mariner a spectacle at the same time as grand as it is admirable'. 'Moreover,' he continued, 'one is sure of finding ... anchorages such that it is impossible to wish for any better whatever may be the nature of one's need for repairs.' Besides, he continued, Adventure Bay did not offer such shelter or endless resources and is situated on 'an island entirely separate from the mainland by the strait we have discovered'.[11] Their discoveries certainly had cut mainland Tasmania down to size.

Aged only 25, Beautemps-Beaupré (henceforth Beaupré) was a brilliant and meticulous hydrographer. He seems to have worked ceaselessly, often in open boats in all weathers and overnight, apparently commanding the willing assistance and respect of the crews. He obviously held a high opinion of his own methods and results, but that cannot be denied. This serious surveyor must have proved a contrasting character in the society of the great cabin to the outgoing, voluble and caustic tongued Labillardière.

In a lengthy and detailed exposition of his hydrographic surveying techniques, which were an appendix to Rossel's 1808 edited version of the journal of d'Entrecasteaux, Beaupré acknowledged his mentors. He had worked for six years constructing marine charts under the distinguished direction of Claret de Fleurieu, minister of marine, and Jean-Nicholas Buache, chief hydrographer in the *Dépôt de la Marine*. Not only was Beaupré well connected, Buache was his cousin. Yet it was the quality and innovative nature of his work rather than personal influence that resulted in a celebrated career crowned with the award of Grand Officer of the Legion of Honour.

Beaupré's techniques were so relevant to nineteenth century maritime surveying that, in 1823, his published account was separated from the Rossel publication and translated into English by Richard Copeland, a Royal Navy Captain, who had the approval of the Lords Commissioners of the Admiralty.[12]

Beaupré faced up to three major problems of maritime surveying in that era, a time when so many new discoveries were being made that virtually the entire Pacific Ocean needed mapping. The first complication was the impossibility of establishing a conventional terrestrial base line if the ship simply sailed past a land mass and nobody set foot ashore. Secondly, there were so many possible errors in dead reckoning (currents, winds, variations in course steered) that it was useless for accuracy. Another quandary was that magnetic compass bearings often were inaccurate. He had experienced these errors while mapmaking in France. His conclusion was warmly supported by Matthew Flinders, who experimented with using the compass on different places on a ship. Flinders quoted Beaupré in support of the unreliability of compass bearings in surveying.[13]

Beaupré's solution was to rely upon astronomical measurements rather than terrestrial bearings, abandoning the use of the mariner's compass. Rossel and his team were involved at this point, using the chronometer to determine their position. Beaupré cited his trigonometrical survey of Santa Cruz Island to exemplify his methodology, reproduced by Copeland in his translation. He acknowledged five days of cooperation from Rossel and Bonvouloir in calculating latitude and longitude from astronomical observations as they sailed near Santa Cruz, while he noted variations in the magnetic needle.[14]

His major innovation was to adopt the reflecting circle for measuring the angular distances from each landmark instead of taking compass bearings. This required many trigonometric calculations and the resulting chart consisted of a network of triangular lines as the framework for his chart of coastlines. He worked exhaustively, immediately drafting a working map, adding careful sketches of coastal features. This procedure meant that each day's observations were consolidated into an easy reference chart, corrected by latitude and longitude observations. A final chart would be prepared for publication in France. As Beaupré wrote: 'If a chart is constructed on the evening of the day of the survey, any errors which may have imperceptibly crept into it … are readily detected.'[15]

A sad footnote is merited to this brilliant hydrography at Santa Cruz. Vanikoro (named Recherche Island by d'Entrecasteaux) was visible and accurately mapped by Beaupré. It was about 64 kilometres distant, the closest that this search was to approach La Pérouse's wreck site. Survivors may have been alive at this time, because recent research has established that some crew must have lived ashore.

Once the ships anchored in Recherche Bay, Beaupré and assistants were on constant duty. He and Jouvency were given the task to survey Port du Nord and take soundings of the depth of water in the bay. A meticulous map resulted, including the anchorages of the two ships and 'jardin', indicating the location of Delahaye's 1792 garden. D'Entrecasteaux acknowledged their chart as drawn with great precision.[16] The chief role of the observatories set up by each vessel was to allow astronomical observations from a solid base to fix longitude and to rate the chronometers. This drew upon lunar tables that set the moon's location at 12-hour intervals and the care that Rossel and his staff lavished upon their observations.

On 26 April Crestin commanded an oared boat that took Beaupré to the southern region of Recherche Bay, where they anchored in the following year. They spent a night in the boat, returning with a sounding record and a 'precisely detailed' plan drawn by the hydrographer.[17] Despite this, the map of the southern harbour published in 1807, is credited to Jouvency, who was entrusted with conducting a more detailed survey during 1793.

Crestin and the two hydrographers set out again on 30 April to reconnoitre the coastline to the north-east. They returned four days later, unfortunately because they had no rations left, thus preventing testing their belief that they had found a passage to the north-east. They had indeed sailed up the D'Entrecasteaux Channel. D'Entrecasteaux correctly suspected that this was a strait and therefore that Adventure Bay was part of an island, separated from Tasmania. It determined him to pursue further survey of a region 'which seemed to offer such great advantages to navigation'.[18] Upon sailing out of the harbour d'Entrecasteaux decided to order a comprehensive survey of the channel and of its islands from Bruny to Maria. According to Labillardière, the D'Entrecasteaux Channel was so named on 17 May 1792.[19]

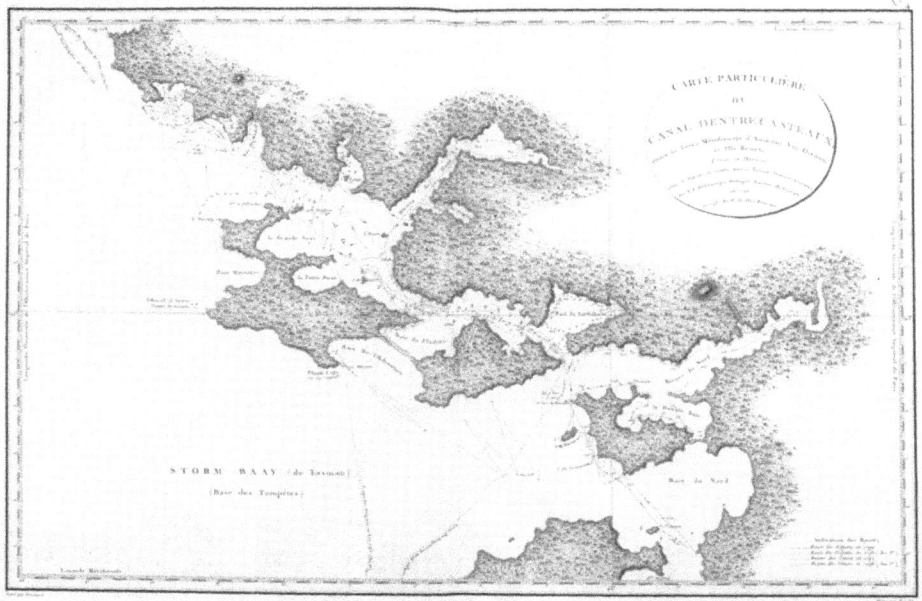

Beautemps-Beaupré's chart of D'Entrecasteaux Channel. National Library of Australia

Beautemps-Beaupré's chart of D'Entrecasteaux Channel showing triangular lines of sight. Flinders praised this as the best survey in any new country. Published in *Atlas du voyage de Bruny-Dentrecasteaux ...*, Depot general des cartes et plans de la marine et des colonies, Paris, 1807. National Library of Australia [map ra82-s6].

The surveyors were busy during these few days in mapping remaining areas, going some distance up the Huon River, named after Kermadec. Beaupré and Rossel combined to fix the location of Observatory Point and the exact position of the southern opening of the strait. This exacting task was finished on 27 May. All astronomical observations, bearings, coastal sketches and soundings made from both vessels were consolidated. 'On this basis a chart of the strait was prepared on board the *Recherche* by Ms Beaupré.' Despite frequent bad weather conditions, this formidable task, which surveyed the hitherto unknown embayed coasts and islands of an area more than 70 kilometres long by up to 30 kilometres broad, was completed within one month.[20]

Both Captains were impressed. In paying tribute to Beaupré, Kermadec wrote: 'The intelligence and care he has brought to this work is an assurance of its great perfection. It is difficult to give an idea of the exactness he has put into all his operations.' D'Entrecasteaux was fulsome in his praise that Beaupré had 'inspired us with the greatest confidence in the work'. 'I could not praise enough [his] zeal and intelligence,' he had observed previously, 'the detailed map he has drafted with the greatest precision ... He has been assisted by all the officers and pilots aboard.'[21]

'The axe had never sounded'

View of Rocky Bay from 1793 watering place, 2006. John Mulvaney

View of Rocky Bay from 1793 watering place. The ships anchored in the centre of this image. John Mulvaney, 2006

During the 1793 visit, d'Entrecasteaux took the opportunity to refine their knowledge of the strait. Having sailed the two craft into the Channel, Beaupré was sent with de Welle to further explore the Huon River and the western side of Bruny Island. Another boat commanded by Willaumez was sent to explore the north-eastern area of the strait. It was then that the Derwent River was located, named by Willaumez as Rivière du Nord. 'I do not believe,' d'Entrecasteaux wrote with gratification, 'that such a large number of excellent anchorages exists in such a small space, anywhere in the world.'[22]

Two decades later, Matthew Flinders provided authoritative and independent evaluation of the quality of the hydrographic survey. His long imprisonment on Ile de France provided him with reasons for denigrating French initiatives, so his praise is all the more to be accepted. This discovery, survey and charting of D'Entrecasteaux Channel is a major criterion in the national status of Recherche Bay, which served as the base for this painstaking survey. Flinders wrote as follows:

> The charts of the bays, ports and arms of the sea at the south-east end of Van Diemen's Land, constructed on the expedition by Mons. Beautemps-Beaupré and assistants, appear to combine scientific accuracy and minuteness of detail, with an uncommon degree of neatness in execution; they contain some of the finest specimens of marine surveying, perhaps ever made in a new country.[23]

ENDNOTES

[1] Duyker and Duyker (eds and trans), *Bruny d'Entrecasteaux: voyage to Australia and the Pacific*, 2001: 2 for list of equipment.

[2] Plomley and Piard-Bernier, *The General*, 1993: 80, 92. For an account of surveying instruments, Pearson, *Great Southern Land*, 2005: 74-9; Richard, *Le Voyage de d'Entrecasteaux*, 1986: 103-5.

[3] Labillardière, *Voyage in search of La Pérouse*, 1800: 100, 139.

[4] Duyker and Duyker (eds and trans), *Bruny d'Entrecasteaux: voyage to Australia and the Pacific*, 2001: 46.

[5] Greenhill, *James Cook, the opening of the Pacific*, 1970: 27.

[6] Rossel, *Voyage de d'Entrecasteaux*, 1808, vol. 2: 20.

[7] Lilley and Day, *Eos* 74 (1993): 97-103; Lilley, *Geophysics Down Under* 14 (1991): 5-6; Day, *Australian Geologist* 80 (1991): 6-8.

[8] Rossel, *Voyage de d'Entrecasteaux*, 1808, vol. 2: 20.

[9] Lilley and Day, *Eos* 74 (1993): 97-103; Lilley, *Geophysics Down Under* 14 (1991): 5-6; Day, *Australian Geologist* 80 (1991): 6-8.

[10] Beautemps-Beaupré, *Atlas du voyage de Bruny-d'Entrecasteaux*, 1807.

[11] Plomley and Piard-Bernier, *The General*, 1993: 120, 123 – Kermadec.

[12] Copeland, *An introduction to the practice of nautical surveying*, 1823, translation of Beautemps-Beaupré, 1807.

[13] Flinders, *A voyage to Terra Australis*, 1814, vol. 2: 525-6.

[14] Copeland, *An introduction to the practice of nautical surveying*, 1823: 46.

[15] Ibid.: 53.

[16] Duyker and Duyker (eds and trans), *Bruny d'Entrecasteaux: voyage to Australia and the Pacific*, 2001: 35.

[17] Ibid.: 39.

[18] Duyker and Duyker (eds and trans), *Bruny d'Entrecasteaux: voyage to Australia and the Pacific*, 2001: 40-4; Labillardière, *Voyage in search of La Pérouse*, 1800: 105.

[19] Labillardière, *Voyage in search of La Pérouse*, 1800: 124.

[20] Plomley and Piard-Bernier, *The General*, 1993: 80, 92-3 – logbook entries.

[21] Plomley and Piard-Bernier, *The General*, 1993: 96 – Kermadec; Duyker and Duyker (eds and trans), *Bruny d'Entrecasteaux: voyage to Australia and the Pacific*, 2001: 161, 65.

[22] Duyker and Duyker (eds and trans), *Bruny d'Entrecasteaux: voyage to Australia and the Pacific*, 2001 154.

[23] Flinders, *A voyage to Terra Australis*, 1814, vol. 1: xciii.

Chapter 6: Seeking the Tasmanians

For all Australians the expedition's most significant consequence involved their contact with Tasmanian people. Although this was delayed until 1793, it represented the longest and most intensive racial contact until that time. Previous British meetings at Adventure Bay on Bruny Island did not result in such detailed ethnography or racial interaction.[1] Because most of the contact occurred on the north-eastern peninsula and north to Southport Lagoon, these occasions of mutually friendly interaction provide a prime criterion for the area's National Heritage listing. The evidence offered by the several French observers, combined with the area's archaeological potential, provide contemporary Aboriginal Tasmanians with insight into their cultural heritage and the temperament and bearing of their ancestors two centuries ago.

20 years before the French arrival in Recherche Bay, however, their countryman, Marion Dufresne, stepped ashore at Marion Bay in 1772. Although a slave trader, possibly he was imbued with notions of noble primitive societies, innocent of Western ways, living in a pure state of Nature. A few years earlier, Louis de Bougainville had circumnavigated the world and 'discovered' such people living in the Pacific. He returned to France in 1769, so Marion was familiar with their romantic exploits in Tahiti. 'Everywhere,' Bougainville reported, 'we found hospitality, ease, innocent joy, and every appearance of happiness amongst them.'[2] Innocent joys or not, their experiences supported current Rousseauesque notions of a surviving age of noble primitivism independent of the corruption introduced by European society.

Even though Marion Dufresne acted the part, ordering two crew members to strip naked and emerge from the surf as 'natural men' to face the agitated Tasmanians, the ruse proved temporary. Calm ended with the approach of a second boat, which alarmed the onlookers. In the ensuing fracas a Tasmanian was shot and others presumably were wounded.[3] The era of the peaceful interactions may have ended abruptly on this distant beach in 1772, but both French and British attitudes to 'undiscovered' peoples remained essentially humanitarian and philosophically concerned with 'Natural Man'.

While Bougainville's crews were experiencing Tahiti's sexual allurements in 1768, James Cook received instructions from the Royal Society on his behaviour in the Pacific. He should 'exercise the utmost patience and forbearance with respect to the Natives … and to restrain the wanton use of Fire Arms. To have it still in view that shedding the blood of these people is a crime of the highest nature: — They are human creatures, the work of the same omnipotent Author.'[4]

At the same time, at a distinctly pragmatic level, he was to 'carefully observe the Nature of the soil, and the Products thereof … specimens of each … seeds of Trees, Fruits and Grains ... that we may cause proper Examination and Experiments to be made of them. You are like wise to observe the Genius, Temper, Disposition and number of the Natives ...'.[5]

The instructions provided for La Pérouse and d'Entrecasteaux could have been lifted from the same manual. High-minded opinions on restraint to be shown to native populations were accompanied by precise details of what should be mapped, studied and collected. In the case of New Guinea, for example, 'everything is to be investigated, and everything is to be done'.[6]

D'Entrecasteaux, according to the King's orders, was:

> to recommend to every person among the crews, to live in a good understanding with the natives, to endeavour to conciliate their friendship by a proper way of acting and respect; and must forbid them ... ever to employ force ... On every occasion ... act with great mildness and humanity ... His Majesty will look upon it as one of the most successful parts of the expedition that it may be terminated without costing the life of a single man.[7]

That events in Paris would cost the king his own life, is one of the ironies of these instructions.

It is evident that during the late eighteenth century, both British and French humanitarian and romantic views of new lands were linked with the growth of scientific rationalism, which stressed empiricism. Even Marion Dufresne felt curious concerning the pigmentation of the dead Tasmanian, so they washed his body and found that 'it was only smoke and dirt which made him look so dark' — he was a noble savage no longer, but an experimental item.[8] The empirical work by the d'Entrecasteaux personnel is described later. Reflecting upon the subsequent Baudin expedition in Tasmania during 1802, Brian Plomley concluded:

> To the explorers, the Tasmanians were specimens of natural history rather than people ... It was scientific curiosity, in fact, that did all the damage, because it condemned the various native races to be thought of as strange species rather than as people.[9]

Whether this assessment justifiably applies to the events at Recherche Bay during 1792–93 is a matter for the reader's evaluation.

The notion that the Pacific Ocean was a contemporary reproduction of a Greek Arcadia populated with gentle people, took a severe blow with Cook's bloody death in Hawaii, and a less enobling, romantic approach might have been expected. But in revolutionary France this was not so. While both officers and savants at Recherche Bay were at first wary of attack from the inhabitants, they soon adjusted to conditions in this peaceful forested landscape. At the conclusion of their visits, d'Entrecasteaux was pleased to note: 'The encounters we had with them later demonstrated that they are kind, without mistrust.'[10]

To their vexation, the Tasmanians remained unseen during most of their 1792 sojourn. Wherever expeditioners moved they saw ample proof of occupancy, including hearths, discarded utensils and artefacts, brush shelters, shell refuse, distant smoke and many tracks, which they followed to negotiate thick woodland. Yet the people remained concealed.

This was a behavioural practice common to this region. When Tobias Furneaux anchored in Adventure Bay for five days during 1773, not a single inhabitant appeared. James Cook was there for two days in 1777 before people arrived, while Bligh waited vainly for 11 days in 1788, failing to meet anybody at close quarters before he sailed the *Bounty* on to filmic immortality. Bligh returned in 1792, this time on HMS *Providence*, establishing only a fleeting contact with about 20 people.[11]

When Europeans reached Tasmania the entire island possibly supported no more than 5,000 people. Archaeologists believe that the Tasmanian ancestors had walked there across the continent at least 35,000 years before, but had become isolated by the formation of the stormy Bass Strait as melting ice at the end of the ice age caused sea level to rise. Aboriginal people believe that they originated in Tasmania in Dreaming creation times. In either case, there was no further contact with the mainland for more than 10,000 years. In their long period of separation the people developed superficial physical, cultural and linguistic differences. Early Europeans believed that these characteristics distinguished them as a separate race, which some derived from Africa and others Melanesia. This is not so; they originated from the same ancestral stock as mainlanders.[12]

The records of the d'Entrecasteaux and Baudin expeditions provide much vital data concerning Tasmanian traditional life at the time of contact. A remarkable source was added in 1966, with Brian Plomley's magisterial edition of George Augustus Robinson's journals 1829–34. Its text extends over 1,000 pages, recording Robinson's journeys with Aboriginal people, including his prolonged hike around the island. He visited Recherche Bay in February 1830 and again during March and April 1833, by which time disease and dispossession had decimated the population.

In a report written during 1831, Robinson stated that in the area stretching from Bruny Island, Recherche Bay and north to Port Esperance, 'the aborigines accompanying the expedition were the only ones remaining of that once formidable and numerous people'.[13] Those members of his party included Woorraddy, a man from Bruny Island born around the time of the d'Entrecasteaux expedition, and Truganini, born at Recherche Bay or Bruny

Island in 1812. Artists made them the most painted Tasmanians of their generation.

All these fragmentary historical records allow reconstruction of traditional social life, whose basic social unit was the family. Related groups of families constituted a band, numbering up to 70 or 80 persons. Marriage took place between these bands. According to Robinson, the band name of the Recherche Bay people was Lyluequonny, while Bruny Island was home to the Nuenonne band. Together with perhaps five other D'Entrecasteaux Channel bands north to the Derwent estuary, these people were the most maritime adapted Tasmanians. In recent times they are known as the Palawa. They crossed the waters between the islands and the mainland in craft made of eucalyptus bark lashed together in rolls. The central roll was the largest and lashings were bark strips or rushes. Rather than canoes, they might be termed catamarans: 'a kind of raft or float, consisting of two or more logs [bark rolls] tied together side by side,' as defined by the Oxford English Dictionary.

Saint Aignan and Beaupré examined such a craft on Bruny Island in 1792. It was 'a kind of canoe, flat both above and below, about seven to nine feet long, in the middle three or four feet wide and finishing in a point at the two ends,'[14] where it was tightly bound, in upwardly curved horns. In such craft the Lyluequonny and Nuenonne bands interchanged seasonally, to maximise resource exploitation and cement social life and obligations. During the winter the Recherche Bay people evidently crossed to Bruny Island and the latter returned their visit during summer.

This was a region of marine resource abundance, although it is believed that all Aboriginal Tasmanians avoided one resource that the French avidly pursued. For presumed but unknown cultural reasons, scale fish were never eaten. While in Adventure Bay, Bligh remarked on the plentiful remains of shellfish and crustacea, 'but it is remarkable we never saw any fish bones'.[15] D'Entrecasteaux commented that heaps of shellfish proved that they were a major item of diet. He then observed: 'No fish bones, or fishing or hunting material have been found.'[16] Archaeologists have excavated several sites where fish bones are present only in deposits older than 3,000–4,000 years, so in remote antiquity a cultural taboo may have prevented the eating of fish, and this on an island-wide basis.

The failure of the French to comprehend the cultural mores of the Tasmanians resulted in their decision to teach them the use of fishhooks, donating a supply of hooks, 'congratulating ourselves at having supplied them with the means of diminishing one of the most fatiguing employments of the women'.[17]

The coastal waters abounded in crayfish, other crustacea and shellfish (especially abalone, oysters and mussels) and edible seaweed (bull kelp), while seals were present at Recherche Bay. Mutton birds, their chicks, and swan eggs were seasonally available in great quantity, while possums and wallabies were accessible on land. It must be concluded that this regional diet was more nourishing than that available to the French sailors, and the efforts they made to harvest fish, crayfish and oysters suggest that they knew that they were storing palatable food for the future.

That Tasmanians consumed many other birds may be inferred from those species listed as eaten by the French. Louis Ventenat reported that they ate quail, pigeons, thrush, duck, geese, swans and crows (ravens). D'Entrecasteaux added parrots and pelicans to this tally, saying they were 'good to eat'. Together with abundant fish, he added 'our crews have hardly been without fresh food'.[18]

Given the seasonal round between the mainland and Bruny Island, it therefore seems possible that, during the French stay during the 1793 summer, both the Lyluequonny and Nuenonne people were on the mainland around Recherche Bay, thereby maximising the contact possibilities. On rule-of-thumb estimates of band size of possibly 50, upwards of 150 Tasmanians occupied the Recherche Bay and Bruny Island region during 1793. Sadly, by 1831, they could be counted on the fingers of both hands. It is this rapidity with which traditional culture perished that gives cogency to the French evidence for that penultimate generation living in a pristine landscape. More than that, imbued with Rousseauesque sentiments of goodwill towards native peoples, they actively sought contact, disappointed when the inhabitants eluded them. When they finally met, it was friendship and humanity, not racial superiority that governed their curiosity and attempted objectivity in describing these well-adapted people living in their natural landscape. The contrast between their freedom to roam and the confined and uncomfortable life aboard ship must have impressed itself on all visitors. More people crammed into their two ships than occupied the entire area of Bruny Island and south-eastern Tasmania.

During 1792, the smoke from fires was ever present, but the campsites proved empty, though numerous. 'We found some rudiments of huts in these woods,' Labillardière reported soon after their arrival, 'consisting of a framework made of the branches of young trees, and designed to be afterwards filled up with pieces of bark, which the natives always use to cover the outside of their cabins.'[19] Such shelters were made from intertwined sticks with bark covering, less than a metre and a half high and hemispherical in shape. The framework was semicircular and bent so that sticks were tied together with strands of rush where they met. Piron drew two such huts, but the best portrayal was drawn by George Tobin, of HMS *Providence*, at Adventure Bay in 1792, in which sailors are picnicking.[20]

The French concluded that fire-hollowed cavities in the base of giant eucalypts were human habitations. D'Entrecasteaux measured the girth of one such tree at head height and found that it was eight metres. This assumption is unlikely, although these hollows may have provided opportunistic shelter from rain or wind. Labillardière pointed to shells on the ground in such cavities as proof that people ate there. A natural explanation for their formation seems more likely. As the expedition's carpenters found to their frustration, the heartwood in the most sizeable trees was rotten, so during bush fires the prevailing west wind would result in burning the eastern side of the tree. Expeditioners saw some trees resembling chimneys, as they were totally hollow, yet still alive in the external part of the trunk. Brian Plomley suggested that the cause of the decay was the shallow clay soil in which they grew was incapable of nourishing the entire tree, while fires would bake the clay, making it deceptively resemble an artificially induced floor.[21]

During their excursions, scientists benefited from using Aboriginal paths through the forest.[22] Labillardière described them variously as 'tracks', 'beaten paths', 'well-marked tracks', even 'roads'. During their widespread travels across the north-eastern peninsula and north to Southport Lagoon they encountered numerous hut frames, sometimes several adjacent structures, hearths and other evidence of human presence. No Aborigines were seen at Recherche Bay during 1792. Yet smoke, warm hearths and abandoned utensils and artefacts indicated that people were about, but invisible. A sailor claimed to have seen an Aboriginal running away, but as nobody else in his party saw anyone, Labillardière doubted his claim. D'Entrecasteaux reasonably accepted the sailor's account.[23]

Once the frigates left harbour and anchored during their surveying progress in the Channel, people were seen from the decks. Due to light winds it took four days to clear the northern area, allowing time for landward excursions. When landings were made on the mainland or islands, people were seen on at least six occasions, but they melted into the bush before closer contact became possible. They proved annoyingly elusive.

On 20 May 1792, Saint Aignan and Crestin suddenly came upon an encampment, probably on western Bruny Island. A fire was burning and food prepared but nobody was there. Searching the bush they finally saw two men and a child who immediately vanished. Nearby, Saint Aignan had noticed a kangaroo skin hanging on a tree, so he decided to collect it. It had vanished. Both he and Crestin were near, but they neither saw nor heard the lithe removalist who came so close to them.[24] Waiting for the Tasmanians occupied the entire 1792 visit. The following year was to follow the same pattern until the final week.

Early during the 1792 stay, seamen discovered some human bones in the ashes of a fire. Sensationalists proclaimed cannibalism. Saner opinion, shared by d'Entrecasteaux, Kermadec and Labillardière, interpreted the remains as a cremation burial.[25] Fortunately Huon de Kermadec was interested and told naturalist Riche, who volunteered to inspect the site. It was located 'in a sandy cove of the outer bay' (possibly near Sullivan Point on the peninsula). His report to Kermadec suggests that it was a cremation site, although Riche remained non-committal.[26]

Riche described a well-constructed circular hut, in which were found the bones of a young person, some flesh still adhering. The hut 'was a palace in comparison with all the others,' Riche concluded. This was not a house for the living, but for the dead. It was constructed from stakes held in place by pliable loops and tied with rushes. Rushes and grass walls were covered with sheets of bark. It was almost two metres high and about five metres in diameter, greater dimensions than for normal shelters.

The Baudin expedition found comparable structures on Maria Island in 1802 and they were depicted in much the same design as Riche inspected and described. They were illustrated by their excellent artist Leseur in a useful composite drawing that showed different sections of the structure.[27] It was wigwam-like, with curved poles covered with bark strips pleated in hoops at the top. Below this was a mound of grass held in place by small strips of pliable stems, weighted down at both ends by stones. This entire structure had been built over the cremation ashes. The calcined human bones had been smashed and then inserted into a pit. George Augustus Robinson witnessed a comparable cremation ritual in north-western Tasmania in 1832. On Bruny Island during 1829 he saw another grave where 'there was a heap of ashes and some grass and sticks put on top of them'.[28] Betty Hiatt (now Meehan) published an exhaustive survey of cremation in Tasmania for which the evidence indicates that it was practiced throughout the island.[29]

It is interesting to reflect on the female cremation at Lake Mungo, western New South Wales, dated to about 42,000 years ago.[30] This woman had been cremated, her bones deliberately smashed and her calcined remains buried in a pit. Future archaeological research must investigate whether this ancient burial rite reached Tasmania with the original settlers. So far, it is known that cremation took place at West Point, north-western Tasmania around 1,800 years ago.[31]

It was typical of d'Entrecasteaux that he rejected the cannibalism claims, partly because it was a single example, and even though he had not met any Tasmanians, because it would 'represent an outrage to humankind'. He preferred to believe 'that the savages have a custom of cremating the last remains of the human species'. Following their return in 1793, with experience of the essential human values observed of the inhabitants, d'Entrecasteaux exclaimed: 'Oh. How much we should blush, having suspected them last year of eating human flesh!'[32]

Huon de Kermadec completed their 1792 visit with a comparable uplifting concept of those Tasmanians fleetingly encountered in D'Entrecasteaux Channel. While they appeared 'very dirty,' he concluded, 'their eyes were very fine and expressed sweetness and kindness. During the whole of the interview they laughed continually.'[33] In similar vein, d'Entrecasteaux regretted that their 1793 stay involved so short an experience of Aboriginal life.

> If our stay ... could have been extended, we would have had a real opportunity of obtaining a very interesting insight on the lifestyle of human beings so close to nature, whose candour and kindness contrast so much with the vices of civilization.[34]

ENDNOTES

[1] See Mulvaney, *Encounters in place*, 1989: 29-37.

[2] Quoted in Smith, *European vision*, 1960: 25.

[3] Mulvaney, *Encounters in place*, 1989: 29-31.

[4] Quoted in Mulvaney, *Historical Studies* 8 (1958): 136.

[5] Quoted in Smith, *European vision*, 1960: 14.

[6] Duyker and Duyker (eds and trans), *Bruny d'Entrecasteaux: voyage to Australia and the Pacific*, 2001: 290.

[7] Quoted in Dyer, *French explorers and Aboriginal Australians*, 2005: 4.

[8] Mulvaney, *Historical Studies* 8 (1958): 139.

[9] Plomley, *The Baudin expedition*, 1983: 29-37.

[10] Duyker and Duyker (eds and trans), *Bruny d'Entrecasteaux: voyage to Australia and the Pacific*, 2001: 141.

[11] See Mulvaney, *Encounters in place*, 1989: 29-37.

[12] Rhys Jones, in Tindale, *Aboriginal tribes of Australia*, 1974: 317-86.

[13] Plomley (ed.), *Friendly mission*, 1966: 226 n35, 374-6, 709.

[14] Plomley and Piard-Bernier, *The General*, 1993: 133.

[15] Mulvaney, *Encounters in place*, 1989: 37.

[16] Duyker and Duyker (eds and trans), *Bruny d'Entrecasteaux: voyage to Australia and the Pacific*, 2001: 34.

[17] Labillardière, *Voyage in search of La Pérouse*, 1800: 313.

[18] Plomley and Piard-Bernier, *The General*, 1993: 351 – Ventenat; Duyker and Duyker (eds and trans), *Bruny d'Entrecasteaux: voyage to Australia and the Pacific*, 2001: 36.

[19] Labillardière, *Voyage in search of La Pérouse*, 1800: 97, 101, 109.

[20] Illustrated in Mulvaney and White, *Australians to 1788*, 1987: 324.

[21] Labillardière, *Voyage in search of La Pérouse*, 1800: 99-100; Plomley and Piard-Bernier, *The General*, 1993: 349 – Ventenat, 119 – Kermadec; Duyker and Duyker (eds and trans), *Bruny d'Entrecasteaux: voyage to Australia and the Pacific*, 2001: 37.

[22] Eg Labillardière, *Voyage in search of La Pérouse*, 1800: 134, 284, 290, 321; Plomley and Piard-Bernier, *TheGeneral*, 1993: 132.

[23] Duyker and Duyker (eds and trans), *Bruny d'Entrecasteaux: voyage to Australia and the Pacific*, 2001: 36.

[24] Labillardière, *Voyage in search of La Pérouse*, 1800: 123, 127-9, 132, 134.

[25] Labillardière, *Voyage in search of La Pérouse*, 1800: 117; Duyker and Duyker (eds and trans), *Bruny d'Entrecasteaux: voyage to Australia and the Pacific*, 2001: 46; Plomley and Piard-Bernier, *The General*, 1993: 118 – Kermadec.

[26] Plomley and Piard-Bernier, *The General*, 1993: 118 – Riche.

[27] Plomley, *The Baudin expedition*, 1983: 82; Bonnemains, Forsyth and Smith (eds), *Baudin in Australian Waters*, 1988: 50-1.

[28] Plomley (ed.), *Friendly Mission*, 1966: 637-8, 57. He also witnessed other cremation evidence.

[29] Hiatt, *Mankind* 7 (1969): 104-19.

[30] Bowler, et al., *Nature* 421 (2003): 837.

[31] Meehan, *Mankind* 7 (1969): 107.

[32] Duyker and Duyker (eds and trans), *Bruny d'Entrecasteaux: voyage to Australia and the Pacific*, 2001: 46-7.

[33] Plomley and Piard-Bernier, *The Genera*, 1993: 122-3 – Kermadec.

[34] Duyker and Duyker (eds and trans), *Bruny d'Entrecasteaux: voyage to Australia and the Pacific*, 2001: 140.

Chapter 7: Meeting the Tasmanians

When Labillardière and other savants disembarked at Recherche Bay for the second time, the date was 24 January 1793. The frigates were anchored in Rocky Bay, unknown to the British at Sydney. In two days time Sydney Cove would celebrate five years of occupation. The prompt publication and English translation of Labillardière's account in 1800 made an important contribution towards humanising the Tasmanians. Unfortunately that information and the sympathetic attempt at cross-cultural understanding exerted no influence upon Risdon Cove's settlers in 1803. Ironically, that settlement was largely made because of unnecessary concern for French territorial intentions following the d'Entrecasteaux and Baudin explorations in Tasmanian waters.

According to the *Recherche* log, it was on 6 February that Labillardière and Delahaye led a party of four on an overnight excursion to the familiar north-eastern peninsula, returning to their 1792 main botanising field. Labillardière's book gives the date as 8 February, but the log entry is to be preferred. This is corroborated by Delahaye's brief journal.[1]

There is some difficulty in interpreting Labillardière's account, following their departure from the *Recherche* at 5am. He states that they landed at the mouth of the harbour on its western side. As they later had to cross what must be the D'Entrecasteaux River from its west bank, possibly they landed in the vicinity of Ryans Point. As this is a rocky area and they collected oysters, it is a contender. If so, they traversed over three kilometres through the bush, in the vicinity of the future Leprena track, before reaching the 'head of the harbour' presumably at the mouth of the D'Entrecasteaux River. They probably followed a well-trodden Aboriginal trackway which ran from the south coast to Southport Lagoon.[2] They continued up the riverside but were unable to cross it until well upstream, where they crossed on a fallen log. They then headed north-east and after at least another three kilometres they reached 'the great lake,' also described by Delahaye as 'a large lake'. This must be Southport Lagoon and they then walked around its southern margin to the sea.

If this was indeed their day's outing, it was a strenuous one, and they faced a long hike back on the peninsula to reach their collection point, somewhere near the garden (which they visited) on Coal Pit Bight. Little wonder that when evening came Delahaye reported that they were too tired to construct a bough shelter. They simply lay in the open by a fire. Upon that cool summer's night the party passed an untroubled sleep.[3]

While botanising on the following morning, the scientists left the two seamen asleep in camp. When in the bush, armed only with their specimen collecting pruning knives, they heard voices. They prudently returned to camp where the men had muskets. Labillardière's account is calm, but Delahaye's version has them running away 'as fast as we could'. Armed with loaded muskets they then set out to trace the source of the voices.[4]

There was no need for arms and no fear of attack. Labillardière says that he approached the group of men, women and children holding out a biscuit (part of the meagre rations about which he grumbled) to an older man. He accepted it with a 'very good grace' and peaceful race relations were initiated.

This long desired meeting with Tasmanians had at last taken place but, unfortunately, less than a week before the frigates were to sail. The amount of what may be termed observant participation during those few days is remarkable and so, also, is the agreement in the different accounts provided by officers and scientists. Although some of it must have been communicated by Labillardière (d'Entrecasteaux, for example, only mingled with the people once), the independent version by d'Auribeau is testimony to their attempts at objectivity. Resulting from this first week's encounter on the Tasmanian mainland between inhabitants and Europeans is a precious record of Aboriginal culture only 10 years before British settlement overwhelmed traditional ways.

There were 42 persons at this first encounter, seven men, eight women and their children, so at least half a band (or clan) was present, possibly constituting seven families. They appeared fearless and eager to communicate. One piece of intelligence conveyed in mime eased the visitors' concerns and demonstrated the peaceful nature of these presumed savages. During the night, while the French slumbered nearby, the Tasmanians visited, leaving them to sleep soundly. Neither then nor upon any other occasion were objects stolen, a virtue stressed by the French.

Simple gifts were exchanged — a neckcloth and a handkerchief added to the biscuit, while a shell necklace was offered in return. Clothing then followed, presumably a form of charity, because the French could not understand survival in that climate without clothes and they wore plenty because of the chill nights, but were burdened with them during the warm days. Although some people, including women, wore a wallaby or kangaroo skin on their shoulders, their lower body was naked. Nakedness was a feature emphasised by all diarists. Labillardière was amused to see seven girls watching events safely perched high above him on a branch; Delahaye was interested to note that they rejected offers of food and, not surprisingly, 'were surprised to see hot water'. Labillardière made several careful ethnographic observations concerning their beards and 'woolly' hair; skin colour made darker with charcoal powder; and impressive cicatrices, incised, he later learned, with the edge of a mussel shell. He also used his knowledge of exploration journals to remark that unlike those New Hollanders reported to knock out their upper front teeth, they did not follow that custom.[5]

The men had hidden their long spears, retrieving them when the French prepared to leave. According to Delahaye, this was only to entrust them to the women to carry away. The unarmed men escorted the party by the shortest track to the boat station. Before they left, however, Labillardière initiated the earliest episode in Tasmanian ethnographic technology. He encouraged a man to demonstrate spear throwing. The man threw his spear at an indicated target on several occasions with what the French judged to be impressive accuracy. Labillardière's important observation was that the man held the spear high and horizontal, drawing it back three times 'with a jerk, which gave it a very perceptible tremulous movement at each extremity,' when it flew almost 100 paces. The tremulous movement, he believed, accelerated its pace and prolonged its flight. When aimed at the indicated target, his accuracy was impressive, and Delahaye paid tribute to his 'great dexterity at a great distance'.[6]

On their return walk, 'the attentions lavished on us by the savages astonished us,' exclaimed the grateful Labillardière. They cleared the track by removing dead branches or breaking off obstructions — perhaps a normal procedure for keeping paths open? Somewhat to the visitors' irritation they also took them by the arm in slippery areas, as they guided them to the beach. The whole group went on arm-in-arm singing.

When the French and their guides reached the harbour shore, the rowing boat was not waiting. So they decided to visit the 1792 garden, which was close by. Another lesson in Tasmanian comprehension followed. The two botanists left the sailors hoping that they would detain the Aborigines, so they would not harm the prospective vegetable crop (as though they had not visited there previously!). One man, however, insisted on accompanying them. Of course there was no crop, but Labillardière believed that the man distinguished those struggling European plants from native flora. Whatever the meaning of the mime, it is relevant that Labillardière favoured an interpretation that stressed the intelligence and inquisitiveness of the Tasmanian, just as the spear throwing demonstration showed skill.[7]

These sentiments characterised all the French diarists. Their material existence may have been thought primitive, but they had fully sentient minds. As they returned to the ship following an enlightening day, the Tasmanians strode off equally pleased with events, having declined invitations to board the oared boat.

On the following morning a larger party set out to meet the people; fortunately Piron the artist was amongst them. This time they rowed along the shore beyond the port and met the welcoming people on higher land, possibly near Blackswan Lagoon. There were 19 people present, eating shellfish beside three fires.

'The axe had never sounded'

'Aborigines of Van Diemen's Land preparing a meal', ['Sauvages du Cap de Diemen preparant leur repas'], Jean Piron, 1793. National Library of Australia

Aborigines of Van Diemen's Land preparing their meal [Sauvages du Cap de Diemen preparant leur repas], by Jean Piron, 10 May 1793, with friendly fraternisation in action. Engraving by Jacques Louis Copia, 1764-1799, in *Atlas pour servir a la relation du voyage a la recherché de la Perouse*, Paris: Chez Dabo, 1817, Plate 5. National Library of Australia [nla.pic-an20973389]

This extraordinary encounter of racial harmony was eternalised by Piron, whose realistic sketch of the occasion was possibly spoiled by the Paris engraver's emphasis upon classical artistic forms, which exaggerated Piron's classicism. Given the ethnographic accuracy in this image, the background hills and totally unrealistic vegetation must also be the imaginative work of the engraver. Note, however, that the area is clear of brush in marked contrast to the whole of the peninsula today. Presumably this resulted from regular Aboriginal firing.

While classical ideals of bodily stature prevail, there is a remarkable degree of realism in the scene. The setting includes three hearths with crayfish broiling and in the foreground are depicted fine examples of basketry and seaweed water containers. 17 Tasmanians are identifiable, although the sex of some is indeterminate. The probable tally is seven men, five women and five children. Some women are seated with one foot concealing their genital area, a characteristic commented upon by most diarists, so this sketch represents keen ethnographic accuracy.

It is possible to suggest tentative identifications of the French participants, following reading of diaries to ascertain who could have been present. To begin with the figure standing in the rear wearing a naval tricorne hat: D'Auribeau did not attend this meeting, but Ventenat was an enlisted man present, so he would wear a uniform. Before him is a well-dressed figure holding an object in an awkward fashion. He could be whittling wood, demonstrating the use of a knife, as diarists recorded this activity at other times. Surely, however, this is Saint-Aignan playing his violin, even though to identify the object as a violin is questionable. He was there and played to the people, a sound that 'did not please them at all,' remarked La Motte du Portail. He also commented that Saint-Aignan 'can be considered a very good amateur player'.[8] While on Buka Island some months before, his violin had proved popular, so 'at the indifference shown to his performance here,' Labillardière thought Saint-Aignan was mortified. Ventenat played his flute with greater success in audience reaction.[9] It may seem special pleading, but possibly the Parisian engraver was unaware that it was a violin that Saint-Aignan held, so he modified the object. A violin in this setting was unusual.

There is a well-dressed man wearing a brimmed beaver hat standing to the left of the group, in friendly stance with a statuesque Tasmanian. This probably is Labillardière. Also in this group is a figure in cap and pantaloons. Is he French or Tasmanian? Labillardière provides the likely answer. He recounted that Piron expressed a 'wish of having his skin covered like theirs with the powder of charcoal'. His body was soon blackened by an obliging man, who even blew dust from Piron's eyes. Much to the delight of the charcoal artist, 'Piron was presently as black as a New-Hollander,' so Piron surely placed himself by his friend Labillardière and his new-found body painter, whose hand appears blackened from his labour.[10]

Such carefree fraternisation indicates the degree of informality and equality that typified the humanising spirit of the occasion. So too does the fact that a nursing mother allowed various Frenchmen to hold her baby. This incident also is included by Piron. A man holds a baby aloft. As sailors were present, it may be a crew member. On the other hand his clothing and cap look superior to a common seaman's. As Riche was present, he seems a likely candidate for Piron's eye.[11] Riche was tubercular, so is this portrayal symbolic of the transmission of deadly diseases, which, by 1831, according to George Augustus Robinson, had reduced the populations of Bruny Island and south-eastern Tasmania to a handful? In 1793 there probably were 150 inhabitants. What then of the remaining well-dressed figure on one knee to the right of the scene? In a letter to Zélie, La Motte du Portail described the meeting, so he is the likely person. With his gaze upon a woman with whom he is conversing, Zélie might feel displeased, had she been told.

'The axe had never sounded'

PECHE DES SAUVAGES DU CAP DE DIEMEN.

'Tasmanians preparing a meal from the sea', ['Peche des sauvages du Cap de Diemen'], Jean Piron, 1793. National Library of Australia

Tasmanians preparing a meal from the sea [Peche des sauvages du Cap de Diemen]. Note the role of women in food collection. Captain D'Auribeau commented on the accuracy of Piron's sketch. Engraving by Jacques Louis Copia, 1764-1799, in *Atlas pour servir a la relation du voyage a la recherché de la Perouse*, Paris: Chez Dabo, 1817, Plate 4. National Library of Australia [nla.pic-an8953914]

At the next meeting Piron again used his artistic skills to picture an incident that illustrates Tasmanian economic and social life. The occasion probably took place in Quiet Cove, then another open area. Gathered around 10 fires, according to witnesses, were 10 men, 14 women and 24 children, 12 of each sex.[12] This tally of 48 people was common to both Labillardière's and du Portail's accounts. It suggested to them that each monogamous family had its own hearth. Saint-Aignan again played his violin to an even less appreciative audience, who placed their hands over their ears.[13] D'Auribeau was present at this gathering and offered the comment on Piron's sketch of the scene: that 'the drawing ... of each particular individual, the whole meeting during the meal, the fishing etc — the truth, the naturalness that this clever artist has had the talent to achieve in every respect'.[14]

The special attraction was the preparation and eating of a meal. Food freshness was the keynote, because the women dived for crayfish, shellfish and edible seaweed, placed them on the coals and soon all were consumed. The women also maintained the fires. As the female divers stayed under the cool water for twice the time that the French thought possible, then had to prepare the meal, many attempts were made to influence the men to help, but to no avail. This visual and written account of the female role in food procurement was detailed, more so than most nineteenth-century observers, who stressed the male hunting role in mainland society. The women's activities, in contrast with the men, who simply waited for the food to be caught and cooked, shocked the mores of French culture. 'We witnessed a frightful scene,' Joseph Raoul and du Portail reported.[15] He simply deplored the women diving to catch the meal, then having to cook it, while the men sat and waited. Nothing frightful had transpired.

Quiet Cove, 2006. John Mulvaney

Quiet Cove, where the sea food harvesting may have taken place, as rocks are depicted in Piron's sketch. Note the thin band of rocks and the dense vegetation cover, whereas in Piron's image the land is open. Was this due to Aboriginal firing practices? Photograph by John Mulvaney, 2006

Piron's humans observe classical statuesque proportions, although these features possibly were exaggerated by the engraver for their publication. They also reflect the virtues held by the French republicans of the era when Piron left France. To quote Bernard Smith's categories of virtue: 'Simple in his needs and desires, self-disciplined, courageous, and with great capacity for endurance,'[16] symbols of freedom and romantic perfectibility. Piron's Tasmanians exemplified hard primitivism, as opposed to the soft, languorous, sensuous Polynesians depicted in the art and literature of the Cook era. Piron's people were described by Bernard Smith as 'dry, wiry natives'. All the diarists appear to support such characterisation and, unlike Polynesia, there were no abandoned sexual liaisons. Piron's art is one further cultural factor in the Recherche Bay situation. These people were type specimens of noble savages in the state of hard primitivism. His females in this cross section of activities preparing this one meal are frozen in time, as they catch and cook shellfish and crayfish. An archaeological midden may be visualised accumulating from the ashes mixed with discarded shells and food debris.

Most diarists emphasised the desire shown by the Tasmanians to know the sex of each visitor, because the male imbalance worried them. Consequently sailors were emboldened to exhibit their gender, with Tasmanians concentrating upon young and beardless sailors. They were disturbed to find that they were males also. La Motte du Portail, evidently no longer in doubt concerning her gender, could not resist a sneer that had Louis Girardin dared to come ashore for inspection, 'they would have come across what they wished to find'.[17]

In the midst of such amicable relations, only one incident appears to have jarred feelings. Three sailors attempted to gain sexual favours from two girls, but they fled onto rocks to escape. D'Entrecasteaux was pleased to conclude at the end of their visit that 'no indiscretion was committed'. This probably was correct, as only one sailor, who was disbelieved, claimed to have had sex. It was a remarkable record of restraint amongst 200 men, contrasting greatly with contemporary mores in Polynesia. D'Auribeau made a special point of acknowledging the crew's behaviour, though 'surrounded by naked women and enjoying great freedom'.[18] Gregory Dening's reflections on the meetings between European sailors and Polynesians are appropriate to these first encounters in Tasmania:

> the marginal space between prehistory and history where the encounters between indigenous people and intruding empires created what I have since called the ethnographic moment, that moment in which confrontation with otherness leads to depiction not only of the other but of self.[19]

All observers emphasised the family as the focus of life. Considerable discussion ensued as to whether polygamy was the rule (as philosophically expected in a 'primitive' society), but the evidence suggested monogamy, the strength of 'marriage' and the devotion of parents to their children. D'Auribeau took this matter so seriously that, 'I asked several officers from the two frigates to study the matter carefully … but most of the observers saw no sign at all of polygamy … I merely report the result of my observations and those of almost all the officers.' It is interesting to note that he did not trust republican opinion by asking the advice of savants, but otherwise his objectivity is impressive.[20]

The more the two races became acquainted, the greater the emphasis on the essential humanity of the Tasmanians and their loving treatment of children, the sharing of food and their good humour. 'We never saw in them a trace of bad temper,' d'Entrecasteaux reflected. He went on to recount 'a roguish trick' played by a young man, who took away and hid a bag of shellfish collected by a sailor. After he had searched for it in vain, it was returned, to be found in its original place. This 'waggish trick' created much merriment for the perpetrator, Labillardière reported. He also told of a talkative young girl who walked with him babbling incomprehensible things, but everyone was happy.[21]

The objectivity of these observers, even when they were puzzled by actions, added a significant collection to the meagre store of ethnographical knowledge of contact period Tasmanians. While d'Auribeau appears to have been unpopular with Labillardière and du Portail, what he drew from his limited meetings with the Tasmanians is impressive, both for its scope and its sympathy. As with the monogamy question, d'Auribeau verified his information. Collecting a word list, he tested the data:[22] 'we carefully compared' and repeated words to informants, 'and they understood most of the words very well'. He realised that French pronunciation must have proved difficult to comprehend, just as a Frenchman who reads English may not be understood in conversation with an Englishman. He found that Tasmanians could not articulate 'f' and substituted 'p'. On the other hand, Ventenat concluded: 'there are very few consonants and the sounds T and F are unknown, it being difficult to pronounce them'.[23]

D'Auribeau provided a sensible account of physical anthropology. He made 14 measurements to describe male and female subjects and estimated the ages of the 48 people whom they met. Two men he judged to be older than 70 and four women were between 50 and 60. All the rest were younger than 50. He found that they expressed a definite preference for red cloth over white or blue cloth as presents. Wisely, he concluded that 'we spent too short a time with these good natives to be able to discover any religious beliefs. Moreover I hold that metaphysical ideas are not transmitted with the same ease as are physical ones and that it is only after a long sojourn among a people that one can determine something in that connection.'[24]

It was a potential loss for the history of anthropology that this thoughtful man died within the year. Had he survived to write an account of his voyage and the 'natural goodness' of these people, it could have assisted dispelling much nonsense later written about Tasmanians.

The French were deeply impressed with the bearing and intelligence of Mara, the sole Tasmanian they enticed aboard *Recherche*.[25] It must have proved a traumatic experience for Mara as he toured the frigate, and sat in the Captain's cabin in the presence of a local ethnographic collection. He was presented with a cock. (Had he not indicated that he would kill and eat it, d'Entrecasteaux also would have supplied a breeding hen). The crew later took their pet monkey and a kid goat ashore to the amusement and wonderment of the people, who preferred the kid's company to that of the monkey. Of all the sailors, the one they made a fuss about was a 'negro', presumably a black African, whom they greeted warmly.[26]

With all these informal harmonious happenings, Stephanie Anderson is correct to conclude that, 'looking back on it now in the light of indigenous / settler relations in Australia, it is hard not to romanticise it as a moment in time when an encounter across European and Aboriginal culture succeeded'.[27]

The French made strenuous efforts to establish a word list. Labillardière's vocabulary included 83 words. However, Plomley and Piard-Bernier consolidated a vocabulary of 155 words from all the French diarists. Words were carefully obtained, as d'Entrecasteaux explained: 'We have made them repeat the same word several times; and after they had repeated it, they would designate the object we had requested them to name. We have asked the same question of several of them; and we have used the same means to ensure that the pronunciation was correct.'[28]

Joseph Raoul, the second pilot on *Recherche*, produced a reliable word list, which he gave to d'Auribeau. Upon meeting the same people for a second time, he related, 'I profited by their willingness to correct some of the words I had collected from them ... and to gather some more. Because I had an opportunity to check the meaning I am sure that they are accurate; and I have only recorded words which I heard clearly and were repeated several times.'[29]

D'Auribeau thought that their speech was 'crisp and lively,' but found that some words which he pronounced distinctly, Tasmanians could not repeat — '*français* and *d'Entrecasteaux* were among them. They said *anglais* extremely well, likewise the names of almost all the officers. It seemed to me that they were unable to articulate the *f* and that they substituted *p* for it.'[30]

Collecting words was not all plain sailing. La Motte du Portail regretted that, 'because of the rapidity with which they pronounced their words and because of their general lack of concentration I was often obliged to shake them by the arm ... so as to make them remember that I was with them'. D'Auribeau also commented on the many distractions that made it difficult to maintain an interview.[31]

Ventenat, priest and flautist, was interested in their song and dance. At one of the meetings he observed:

> Their dance consists of raising one foot behind them, touching the head with the hand, then they bend the body down and straighten up in turn, the movements being made quite violently. Their voice is sonorous, pleasant and agreeable. When they sing they only have two tones, which are pitched between B and G.[32]

Ventenat was realistic in his approach to language and the ease of misunderstanding a meaning based upon signs. 'They articulate in the throat and speak very rapidly,' he concluded. 'There are few consonants, and the sounds T and F are unknown, it being difficult to pronounce them.'

Some of the vocabularies may have been derived through songs, for both the French and Tasmanians sang, the former lustily. Labillardière 'was singularly struck' with the modulation of their singing. He drew an analogy with the tunes of Arab music, with which he would have been familiar from his time botanising in Syria. 'Several times two of [the girls] sung the same tune at once, but always one a third above the other, forming a concord.'[33] La Motte du Portail thought that 'the women often sang among themselves, but also very softly and in a very sad manner'. 'As for our songs,' he reported, 'they seemed to listen to them with pleasure.'[34]

Whatever the linguistic merits of this combined vocabulary, it was a sizeable list from a single area, a commendable attempt by eighteenth century standards. When they anchored at Adventure Bay in 1793, the explorers found that the Bruny Islanders understood their words, which they correctly concluded not only established their common language, but that it proved that their words had real meaning.[35] This pioneer vocabulary is not referred in the linguistic survey by Bob Dixon (1980). Until the vocabulary was consolidated by Plomley, however, the words made a less impressive list, notwithstanding the trouble taken to collect them. Thanks to the general care taken by officers and savants to observe the Tasmanians with objectivity and sympathy, a remarkable corpus of information resulted from this cultural encounter.

It is time to reflect upon this momentous and friendly encounter for human history. Since their arrival in southern Tasmania at least 35,000 years ago, the Tasmanians had been isolated from all outside human contact for a period of between 10,000 and possibly 14,000 years. Yet their bearing surely reflected those values that are the criteria of humanity. It is not unreasonable to conclude that their ancestors brought this culture with them on their long migration. They spoke fluently and in lively manner, communicating meaning to the French newcomers. They sang, danced and showed their trust, affection and consideration when they grasped the visitors' arms. The French already had inferred that they had solicitude (or fear) for deceased kin in the form of cremating their dead. These were hardly the characteristics of sub-human and unintelligent savages. These distinguishing traits of conversational jollity and adaptability stamped these remote people for their French observers as fully sentient *Homo sapiens*, whereas many later colonists assumed otherwise.

The limitations of time and comprehension were understood by d'Entrecasteaux, who 'regretted that we have only met up with them at the end of our sojourn'.[36] He was not to know that within 40 years the Recherche Bay and Bruny Island communities would have virtually ceased to exist.

ENDNOTES

[1] Plomley and Piard-Bernier, *The General*, 1993: 159 – *Recherche* log; Labillardière, *Voyage in search of La Pérouse*, 1800: 293; Duyker and Duyker, *Explorations* 37 (2004): 39.

[2] Plomley and Piard-Bernier, *The General*, 1993: 359-60 – Ventenat.

[3] Duyker and Duyker, *Explorations* 37 (2004): 39.

[4] Labillardière, *Voyage in search of La Pérouse*, 1800: 295-6; Duyker and Duyker, *Explorations* 37 (2004): 40.

[5] Labillardière, *Voyage in search of La Pérouse*, 1800: 296-302; Duyker and Duyker, *Explorations* 37 (2004): 40.

[6] Labillardière, *Voyage in search of La Pérouse*, 1800: 300; Duyker and Duyker, *Explorations* 37 (2004): 41.

[7] Labillardière, *Voyage in search of La Pérouse*, 1800: 301.

[8] Plomley and Piard-Bernier, *The General*, 1993: 339 – du Portail.

[9] Labillardière, *Voyage in search of La Pérouse*, 1800: 303; Plomley and Piard-Bernier, *The General*, 1993: 361 – Ventenat.

[10] Labillardière, *Voyage in search of La Pérouse*, 1800: 304; on Riche as a disease carrier, Poulson, *Recherche Bay*, 2004: 14.

[11] Plomley and Piard-Bernier, *The General*, 1993: 361 – du Portail.

[12] Plomley and Piard-Bernier, *The General*, 1993: 342 – du Portail.

[13] Labillardière, *Voyage in search of La Pérouse*, 1800: 308.

[14] Plomley and Piard-Bernier, *The General*, 1993: 283 – d'Auribeau.

[15] Plomley and Piard-Bernier, *The General*, 1993: 305-6, cf. 341 – du Portail.

[16] Smith, *European vision*, 1960: 110.

[17] Plomley and Piard-Bernier, *The General*, 1993: 340 – du Portail.

[18] Duyker and Duyker (eds and trans), *Bruny d'Entrecasteaux: voyage to Australia and the Pacific*, 2001: 146; Plomley and Piard-Bernier, *The General*, 1993: 284 – d'Auribeau.

[19] Dening, in Griffiths and Bonyhady, *Prehistory to politics*, 1996: 88.

[20] Plomley and Piard-Bernier, *The General*, 1993: 283 – d'Auribeau.

[21] Duyker and Duyker (eds and trans), *Bruny d'Entrecasteaux: voyage to Australia and the Pacific*, 2001: 147; Labillardière, *Voyage in search of La Pérouse*, 1800: 309.

[22] Plomley and Piard-Bernier, *The General*, 1993: 280-85 – d'Auribeau.

[23] Plomley and Piard-Bernier, *The General*, 1993: 363 – Ventenat.

[24] Plomley and Piard-Bernier, *The General*, 1993: 283 – d'Auribeau.

[25] Plomley and Piard-Bernier, *The General*, 1993: 369 – du Portail.

[26] Plomley and Piard-Bernier, *The General*, 1993: 369 (the cock), 287 (negro) – Féron.

[27] Anderson, *Aboriginal History* 24 (2000): 222.

[28] Labillardière, *Voyage in search of La Pérouse*, 1800, appendix: 19-20; Duyker and Duyker (eds and trans), *Bruny d'Entrecasteaux: voyage to Australia and the Pacific ...*, 2001: 148.

[29] Plomley and Piard-Bernier, *The General*, 1993: 307 – Raoul.

[30] Plomley and Piard-Bernier, *The General*, 1993: 280 - d'Auribeau.

[31] Plomley and Piard-Bernier, *The General*, 1993: 305 – du Portail; p. 280 – d'Auribeau.

[32] Plomley and Piard-Bernier, *The General*, 1993: 363 – Ventenat.

[33] Labillardière, *Voyage in search of La Pérouse*, 1800: 305.

[34] Plomley and Piard-Bernier, *The General*, 1993: 306, 302 – du Portail.

[35] Duyker and Duyker (eds and trans), *Bruny d'Entrecasteaux: voyage to Australia and the Pacific*, 2001: 153.

[36] Ibid.: 140.

Chapter 8: An Archaeological Heritage

When an archaeologist contemplates the accounts by the diarists during their two visits to Recherche Bay, his or her eyes should light up, just as the Tasmanians' must have done upon receipt of their gifts. The area around Recherche Bay, particularly the north-east peninsula and the Cockle Creek area, offer great opportunities to document both the French occupation and the racial encounter.

The possibilities for excavating the French presence are obvious. Investigations should cover the area of the observatory and the industrial activities near Bennetts Point during 1792. Action should also be directed to the Cockle Creek occupation in 1793. The site of the supposed garden is an essential area to sample, while the seabed beneath the two anchorages offers potential.

At the time of writing, archaeological investigations are proposed by Dr Jean-Christophe Galipaud. Aboriginal Tasmanian evidence would consist of two chief sources of evidence: their occupation sites and European objects given to them by the French. In the first place, the sources all stress the concentration upon shellfish and crustacea as Aboriginal food sources. Their meals were cooked over small hearths. Over time, the ash would mingle with discarded shells, crab claws and the like, to form accumulations which archaeologists call middens. Labillardière wrote of such middens when he referred to 'the heaps of shells which we found near the seashore'. As he also described, occupation occurred at certain places, presumably close to the food source, water supplies and shelter, as depicted in Piron's sketch of a meal. At one northerly site on the ocean coast, 'it appears that this spot is much frequented, as fourteen fire-places were discovered'.[1] 14 hearths in contemporary use on a site visited, say, every year, would accumulate a substantial midden.

Archaeologists therefore need to undertake an intensive site survey, concentrating on a search for middens. Not all archaeological evidence needs to be adjacent to the sea or lakeshores. There is a possibility that traces of bark and brush shelter sites, associated with hearths, still exist. Then there is the frequent reference to Aboriginal paths, tracks or 'roads' that the French followed. Louis Ventenat reported that tracks were rarely found more than about two kilometres from the sea, including one major track that ran at least 16 kilometres from Southport Lagoon to Southeast Cape.[2] Aborigines avoided densely forested areas according to the French and this has been claimed as making it impossible for them to cross the north-east peninsula. A reading of the diaries establishes that such crossings were made. On their journey from Southport Lagoon to the harbour, when escorted by Tasmanians, Labillardière reported that the

Tasmanians made rest stops.[3] There remains the slight possibility that trackways, artefacts and hearths may be found inland, at rest stops.

Ventenat made a significant reference to an inferred method of Tasmanian kangaroo hunting that had environmental impact. 'My idea, after much thought about this and having examined the ground carefully, is that one frequently comes across in the interior of the country large open spaces which have been burnt. But by whom? Certainly it is by the natives!'[4] His opinion was that by firing the bush, it drove the fleeing kangaroos into the spears of waiting hunters astride animal paths. Whatever the reasons, his comments must rank as one of the earliest references to ecological changes due to deliberate Aboriginal firing practices, resulting in open land. This is one of the several reasons why the understorey today may be thicker than it was in 1792. Note also, Piron's sketches, which portray open settings in areas that today are thick bush.

It was the gift exchange that occurred during that last week in 1793 that provides such potential for excavations documenting the period of contact. This exchange of European goods took place on a surprisingly large scale, as by their final day together officers, scientists and the entire crews became enthused with gift giving. D'Auribeau remarked 'there was not one of us (without exception) who did not give them something of his own'.[5]

These goods included the conventional 'trinkets for the natives', such as mirrors, glass beads, bracelets, coloured cloth and handkerchiefs.[6] Like James Cook at Adventure Bay, they were also supplied with unspecified medals. D'Auribeau presented medals to eight men.[7] However, the main French intention was pragmatic and humanitarian, to provide tools which made life easier. They provided careful demonstrations to teach their use. There are many references to axes and hatchets. D'Auribeau concluded 'that they preferred the axes above all else, and indeed I really think that the axe is the object from which they can draw the greatest benefit'.[8] D'Entrecasteaux reported with gratification that Mara 'used the axe that had been given to him very promptly and with great skill'. He added, that before such gifts were bestowed, 'none of them had been given without its use being explained'.[9]

Other common items were knives, saws and nails. D'Auribeau is again the most explicit source: 'I showed them at leisure the use of axes, saws, knives, nails, etc.: they understood very quickly — I will even go so far as to say with surprising intelligence. And so they were generally very eager in desiring the objects that I was using.'[10] Labillardière confirmed their adaptability to wielding axes. A tree trunk cut by a Tasmanian was sawed in two, after which 'we made them a present of some handsaws, which they used with great readiness, as soon as we had shown them the way'.[11]

Two other contributions to local technology may not have proved so practical. Noting that the community lacked any fishhooks, they were presented with some and instructed in their use. It was anticipated that this would relieve the women of the exhausting tasks which so upset the French. Such was the cultural barrier to understanding that one wonders whether those hooks were ever applied to fishing, given the apparent taboo on eating fish. It was presumably Mara who was rewarded with a 'burning glass'. A demonstration that the magnifying glass could set fire to shredded bark so impressed him that he turned the lens on his thigh, with painful results.[12]

Two further items merit archaeological attention. Because of the maritime environment, it is likely that the salty conditions would rust the iron objects presented, so that may not survive intact. This would not apply to the earthenware pot, the 'small glassware' or 'the bottles we gave them and which were hidden in an instant'.[13] Also, what of the gift of a bottle of wine?[14] These objects broken and used as substitutes for stone tools would survive.

Following shore leave for many crew members of both ships to enable the last meeting with the Tasmanians, Gunner Jean-Louis Féron, from *Recherche*, provided a useful clue to alternative gift giving. 'Each one vied with the rest in giving presents and removing his clothes for these friendly natives,' he recorded.[15] Lieutenant Saint Aignan even presented his jacket to an old man.[16] The reality of archaeological relevance is that the women proved indifferent to gifts of clothing, which they handed to their children. These children busied themselves cutting off any buttons, using their newly acquired knives. 'We gave them presents,' wrote pilot Joseph Raoul, 'but we saw that they were quite indifferent to all the trifles we gave them, even dropping them here and there.'[17] 'The small children who had been given knives entertained themselves by cutting the buttons off our clothes,' remarked d'Entrecasteaux.[18]

To conclude this shower of gifts, the reflections of d'Entrecasteaux on their final meeting are appropriate:

> Most members of both crews were ashore, competing with one another in giving more garments to their new friends, who were attired with every type of cloth. Medals, bells, mirrors, beads, etc. hung around their necks. They looked like real carnival caricatures; besides, these objects made little impression on them.[19]

Readers are provided with scenes of lavish gift giving. In return it is inferred that the French were offered food and that aboard the *Recherche* were spears, baskets and kangaroo skin cloaks, presumably collected from the Tasmanians.[20] They made a deep impression upon Mara when he saw them aboard ship. Buttons, medals and beads were presumably soon scattered and lost. To judge from the accounts already quoted, many were discarded near the sites where they were presented. This provides the middens on the peninsula with added meaning, because such durable objects may be excavated there. This desire for buttons was commented on in 1802 by Baudin.[21] Again, they were cut off clothing. One woman wore a locket of an English penny and a metal button.

There was at least one exchange that was of a mythological nature. Its occasion was a carving on a tree. A gunner from *Espérance* carved an evidently realistic human head. From the context of Labillardière, it probably was on the peninsula. Labillardière was walking in the company of a girl when they came upon it. She was 'surprised' to see it, then pointed to and named the various anatomical features. It seemed a matter-of-fact occasion.[22]

It recurred in different psychological mode in 1831, when George Augustus Robinson visited Recherche Bay. Woorrady, whose land was Bruny Island, told Robinson of a mythological being named Wraeggowraper, a huge, ugly and bad spirit, a harbinger of death. He became specific: 'There is large tree at Recherche Bay on which is cut the head of a man in large size … that the natives call Wraeggowraper and that children cry when they see it, that the native men destroyed it, and that this was done by the first white men.'[23] This suggests that despite French satisfaction at their encounter, Tasmanians recognised this as a truly fatal contact.

Here is a hint that Tasmanian minds were fertile, as the French would have agreed. Only 38 years had elapsed since the carving was made. It is helpful to compare two other intellectual transfers which took place following the British settlement at Risdon in 1803. Dogs were adapted into Aboriginal society and within a decade had become valued items of exchange, while packs of dogs lived with the people. It is relevant that on Tasmania's west coast by 1832 dogs had been incorporated into mythology. Significantly, this included a ferocious dog which devoured humans wearing clothes. Dances also were invented depicting dogs. All these incorporations were documented by George Augustus Robinson and imaginatively retrieved by Rhys Jones in a brilliant article in 1970.[24]

Except for one meeting on the south-western shore of Recherche Bay upon the day the ships sailed, all other contact episodes took place on the peninsula extending up to Southport Lagoon, in the area listed today as a Wildlife Conservation Area, but which a bulldozed track now traverses. It is a heritage tragedy that this track allows mass access to the Conservation Area of destructive 4-wheel drive vehicles. From the above recital, it is evident that in the event of any harvesting of timber on the peninsula, especially if modern mechanised harvesting techniques are employed, archaeological sites would be destroyed and the context of artefacts would be disturbed — an irretrievable loss to Tasmania's heritage.

Apart from the later journals of George Augustus Robinson, containing vital data concerning the displaced people of 40 years later, the d'Entrecasteaux records of the life and times of the first substantial mainland contact are a priceless archive. Contemporary Tasmanians are presented with evidence that was set down as objectively as possible by uncomprehending but sympathetic newcomers. Above all, the keynote of all the observers is the simple humanity of these people, whose family life was seen to exude love, fun and intelligence. Contrast these several accounts with later British descriptions of Aboriginal life and the French acceptance of friendly humanity stands out. That is why Recherche Bay has great symbolic value as a cultural landscape for all Australians, but particularly Aboriginal Tasmanians.

In my opinion, this racial interaction and resulting archive is the prime evidence supporting placing this area on the National Heritage List. Earlier chapters reviewed further criteria — the location of pioneering geomagnetic studies; coastal surveying of supreme excellence; botanical collections which still survive, which include the type specimens of Australian flora, including *Eucalyptus globulus* (blue gum) and heath, now the floral emblems respectively of Tasmania and Victoria. Then there are the cultural associations — a major base for the d'Entrecasteaux expedition, facilitating the French contribution towards European discovery and charting of Australia. Labillardière, a significant eighteenth-century botanist, who knew Sir Joseph Banks and published the first major corpus of Australian flora, is another associated figure of historical significance. It is to Labillardière and the fortunes of his collection that attention is now directed.

ENDNOTES

[1] Labillardière, *Voyage in search of La Pérouse*, 1800: 121, 127.

[2] Plomley and Piard-Bernier, *The General*, 1993: 359-60 – Ventenat.

[3] Labillardière, *Voyage in search of La Pérouse*, 1800: 300.

[4] Plomley and Piard-Bernier, *The General*, 1993: 359.

[5] Plomley and Piard-Bernier, *The General*, 1993: 279 – d'Auribeau.

[6] Plomley and Piard-Bernier, *The General*, 1993: 285, 339.

[7] Plomley and Piard-Bernier, *The General*, 1993: 279.

[8] Plomley and Piard-Bernier, *The General*, 1993: 280 – d'Auribeau.

[9] Duyker and Duyker (eds and trans), *Bruny d'Entrecasteaux: voyage to Australia and the Pacific*, 2001: 147.

[10] Plomley and Piard-Bernier, *The General*, 1993: 280.

[11] Labillardière, *Voyage in search of La Pérouse*, 1800: 313.

[12] Labillardière, *Voyage in search of La Pérouse*, 1800: 313; Plomley and Piard-Bernier, *The General*, 1993: 339, 364.

[13] Labillardière, *Voyage in search of La Pérouse*, 1800: 127; Plomley and Piard-Bernier, *The General*, 1993: 339, 364.

[14] Plomley and Piard-Bernier, *The General*, 1993: 354.

[15] Plomley and Piard-Bernier, *The General*, 1993: 287 – Féron.

[16] Plomley and Piard-Bernier, *The General*, 1993: 285.

[17] Plomley and Piard-Bernier, *The General*, 1993: 304 – Raoul.
[18] Duyker and Duyker (eds and trans), *Bruny d'Entrecasteaux: voyage to Australia and the Pacific*, 2001: 146.
[19] Duyker and Duyker (eds and trans), *Bruny d'Entrecasteaux: voyage to Australia and the Pacific*, 2001: 145.
[20] Plomley and Piard-Bernier, *The General*, 1993: 284.
[21] Cornell, *The journal of Post Captain Nicolas Baudin*, 1974: 305.
[22] Labillardière, *Voyage in search of La Pérouse*, 1800: 306.
[23] Plomley (ed.), *Friendly mission*, 1966: 374.
[24] Jones, *Mankind* 7 (1970).

Chapter 9: Labillardière's Luck

The d'Entrecasteaux expedition proved almost as forlorn a venture as that of La Pérouse, whom they failed to find. Following their Tasmanian departure in 1793 they sailed within 60 kilometres of Vanikoro where La Pérouse was wrecked, but continued on through the Solomon Islands. Previously, off New Caledonia on 6 May 1793, the tubercular Huon de Kermadec died, ostensibly from fever.

Worse followed on 19 July, when d'Entrecasteaux died from scurvy and related complications. As the senior officer, d'Auribeau took command as they approached eastern Indonesian waters. Rossel commanded *l'Espérance*. In an admiral tribute to the significant role of d'Entrecasteaux, Edward Duyker concluded:

> Over a period of nearly two years he had held his ideologically divided expedition together, often in dangerous and unknown waters, with patience, discipline and exemplary skill as a mariner. It was all to unravel.[1]

Aboard *Recherche*, d'Auribeau, whose record of illness extended across most of their time at sea, was so incapacitated that Lieutenant Crestin (who was to die in Java) was the practical commanding officer until October, when d'Auribeau resumed duties. On 19 October 1793 the ships anchored off Madura, East Java, the crews sickly and debilitated with scurvy. Lieutenant Trobriand set off in a large boat with those men sufficiently fit to man it, to report to the Dutch governor at Surabaya, 40 kilometres away. Trobriand failed to return, but six days later came word that he and his crew were interned as prisoners of war. France was at war, they now heard, with Holland. For the first time in two years they heard news from France — their king had been beheaded in January while they were at Recherche Bay.

The governor gave permission for them to enter Surabaya harbour on condition that they hand over all arms and the rudders of both ships, thereby immobilising them. The sick could receive medical attention and their natural history documents could be retained, but d'Auribeau was instructed to requisition all journals and private papers belonging to the expedition members.[2] Somehow Labillardière concealed and retained his journal from this confiscation although others were lost. Over the next three months, divisions sharpened between the royalist and republican interests, with the royalist officers holding the advantage. So it resulted that d'Auribeau preferred to submit to Dutch demands, while the republicans would have fought or attempted to escape by sailing off — foolhardy given their lack of stores and water. Dutch troops arrested officers named by d'Auribeau, the savants and 32 crewmen. Officers and savants then had to walk to Samarang, 15 wet and muddy days away. Except for Labillardière and Piron, they were then moved to Batavia.

The conscientious gardener Felix Delahaye was more fortunate than his superiors in Java. When on Tonga he collected 200 breadfruit plants, emulating the British Captain Bligh. His aim was to transplant them to the Ile de France. By the time that they arrived in Surabaya only 14 plants survived and this was reduced to 10 when Delahaye moved to Samarang. He doubled that minimum by care and layering, so that plants might strike root and propagate, remaining in Java until January 1797. He then tended his breadfruit plants at sea until he planted them on the Ile de France. There they prospered under his care until he returned to France, bearing his journal and collected plant specimens, which he gave to the museum in Paris. He later became gardener to the empress Josephine. At Malmaison he cultivated some plants which originally were collected on the expedition. On a lake, it is reputed, black swans recalled the wilds of Tasmania.[3] Delahaye, the first European gardener in mainland Tasmania and gardener to Napoleon's empress is an exemplar of social associations with Recherche Bay, which add to the national significance of that place.

A total of 218 men and one woman had sailed from Brest in 1791. Tropical Java proved destructive of French lives. Labillardière believed that before the French were to reach Ile de France, 99 would perish. Louise Girardin was one of those who succumbed to dysentery.[4] The number of deaths by the time they reached France probably increased, so a death rate for the expedition of more than 40 per cent is an indication of the perils of the sea and tropical ports at that period.

In July 1794 those prisoners at Batavia, including Ventenat, Riche and Willaumez, sailed with 383 French sailors, all prisoners, for Ile de France. It was not until March 1795 that Labillardière embarked for that destination. Meantime, d'Auribeau negotiated the sale of the two ships to cover payment of all charges for supplies and other costs incurred in Java. Before d'Auribeau could sign this agreement he died from the effects of dysentery on 22 August 1794. The contract of sale was signed by Rossel who was now, through default, the senior officer and commandant. The sale of these historic craft did not even cover the debt that the expedition owed to Holland.

After various alarms and excursions Labillardière finally sailed, reaching France on 12 March 1796, an absence of four and a half years. This was his first good fortune, because he had survived; the second was that he still possessed his journal, despite later efforts while he was at Samarang to again search for it.[5] The saga of his botanical collections was another story.

It was December 1794 when Rossel, Beautemps-Beaupré, seven other officers and 23 former crew members sailed in a convoy of slow moving Dutch merchantmen. On the *Hougly* Rossel had embarked 92 cases, including 45 cases of d'Entrecasteaux's personal effects. These included ethnographic items, presumably those in his cabin seen during Mara's visit. There also were 37 cases of natural history specimens, which included those seized from Labillardière, Riche and Ventenat and many other cases of documents. The inventory of Labillardière's natural history collections recorded 28 cases of plant specimens.[6] From Cape Town, Trobriand and Saint Aignan travelled on the *Hougly* with the records, while Rossel missed the sailing and took passage on the *Herstellder,* which soon fell behind the large convoy.

As the convoy approached St Helena the *Hougly* was captured by the British 64-gun warship *HMS Sceptre*. Captain Essington demanded that Trobriand hand over the French material, which he refused to do. Ignoring Trobriand, Essington had the cases transferred to the *Sceptre* as a prize-of-war, destination England. As Holland was occupied by France, the Dutch ships were regarded by the British as enemy. A few days later the *Hougly*, now emptied of the expedition's scientific outcome, sank during a storm. Labillardière's luck had continued because Captain Essington transferred the cases to his ship, so saving them.

The captured Dutch ships were shepherded to the mouth of Ireland's Shannon River, where Rossel on the subsequently captured *Herstellder* duly arrived. He found the precious cargo safe, but in the wrong hands.

Labillardière's luck continued in the person of Rossel who interceded in England with the duc d'Harcourt, who was the ambassador for the (now exiled) Louis XVIII at the court of St James He still represented the loyalist lobby. Even before Rossel met Harcourt, however, as he and Captain Essington were preparing to disembark from the *Sceptre*, Prime Minister William Pitt came aboard; surely a very useful contact for a foreign enemy.[7]

Rossel, astronomer, surveyor and eventual leader of the expedition, proved a useful ally at the British Hydrographic Office. He remained in London in self-imposed exile until 1802. It is hardly surprising that this royalist, whose mother had been executed and whose father was killed in battle, preferred London's attention to an uncertain future in Paris. It is clear that Matthew Flinders benefited from Beautemps-Beaupré's charts, which were under Rossel's control. Rossel returned to Paris in 1802 only because the short-lived Peace of Amiens made the risk seem worthwhile.

Upon the arrival of the expedition's cases of natural history specimens, charts and other impedimenta the question of their future was an immediate issue. Harcourt invited Sir Joseph Banks, as President of the Royal Society of London, to view the collections. He did so with deep interest. As representative for Louis XVIII, Harcourt was instructed to offer the collections to Queen Charlotte, consort of King George III, whose palace adjoined the Kew botanical gardens.[8]

Banks wrote an enthusiastic report both as to the size and the quality of the flora and fauna collections, but acted scrupulously in not handling specimens. The

Queen agreed to his suggestion that he select specimens for her from the flora, although she was not interested in samples of other material. He had not made this selection by the time that he received an imploring letter from Labillardière. It was dated 14 April 1796, so it was sent within a month of his landing in France. His letter was an appeal to facilitate the collection's return to Paris. '[O]bilge me by doing all that you can to recover my most right property,' Labillardière pleaded.[9]

That the collection was his personal property conflicted with the initial instructions of the expedition. Since that time, however, a king had been beheaded and so had the government ministers who were responsible for his execution. Revolution, wars and radical changes of government made the fine print of agreements difficult to interpret, so nobody bothered to query Labillardière's brave claims. Banks, the British government and the French authorities found it convenient to expedite this request.

In his encouraging response Banks made an impressive claim for the supremacy of science even during war:

> That the science of two Nations may be at Peace while their Politics are at war is an axiom we have learned from your Protection to Capt. Cook and surely nothing is so likely to abate the unjustifiable Rancour that Politicians frequently entertain against each other as to see Harmony and good will prevail among their Brethren who cultivate science![10]

Labillardière was fortunate to have the right influential nabob in the right place at the right time. By 4 August the Foreign Secretary had approved the return of the collections to France. It remained to placate the Queen for not receiving her promised specimens. Banks did so with diplomatic aplomb, by reassuring her through her Vice-Chamberlain that the 'National character of Great Britain will certainly gain much credit for holding a conduct towards science and scientific men liberal in the highest degree'.[11]

In his published book, Labillardière acknowledged the role which Banks played 'with all the exertions that were to have been expected from his known love of the sciences, I soon had the satisfaction of finding myself again in possession of the requisite materials, for making known to the world the natural productions which I had discovered in the different countries'.[12]

Labillardière had obtained the collections, made by others as well as himself, now acknowledged as his private property, even though they were returned to him at the address of the Paris *Jardin des Plantes*. He had scooped the pool, because not only had his collections arrived but, unlike most of his colleagues, his journal was still in his possession. Unfortunate Deschamps lost not only his collections but also his journal. During those years in which Labillardière prepared the *Voyage*, other potential competitors were either dead or awaiting the return of Rossel, who controlled the other cases of material in London. That is why Labillardière's *Voyage* and two English translations were published during 1800, as the first statement by the d'Entrecasteaux expedition. The official journal of d'Entrecasteaux, edited and added to by Rossel, appeared only in 1808, too late to attract public attention. Meanwhile, Labillardière had issued the first major scientific study of Australian flora. *Novae Hollandiae Plantarum* was issued in parts between 1804 and 1807. The importance of this work, the social association involving Sir Joseph Banks and the primacy of his publications, are further cultural or social associations with Recherche Bay and Australia.

Labillardière retained the invaluable floral collection until his death in 1834. Auctioned to cover his death duties, it was purchased by a British botanist, Philip Barker Webb, who resided in Paris. When Webb died in 1854 he bequeathed his enormous plant collection to the Grand Duke of Tuscany. Labillardière's good fortune continues because his flora, including many Australian type specimens, survives for reference in the Museo Botanico at the University of Florence.[13] Following Denis Carr's excellent study of Labillardière, in *People and Plants in Australia* (1981), Labillardière led 'a charmed life'.

ENDNOTES

[1] Duyker, *Citizen Labillardière*, 2003: 187.

[2] Horner, *Looking for La Pérouse*, 1995: 201. Much of the accompanying information was derived from this source.

[3] Ibid.: 229.

[4] Labillardière, *Voyage in search of La Pérouse*, 1800: lxiii.

[5] Ibid.: 471.

[6] De Beer, *Sciences were never at war*, 1960: 54 for the inventory.

[7] Horner, *Looking for La Pérouse*, 1995: 223-34; Duyker, *Citizen Labillardière*, 2003: 189-202 for the information on the preceding pages.

[8] Duyker, *Citizen Labillardière*, 2003: 203-22.

[9] Horner, *Looking for La Pérouse*, 1995: 241; de Beer, *Sciences were never at war*, 1960: 45-68 for the series of letters.

[10] De Beer, *Sciences were never at war*, 1960: 55.

[11] Ibid.: 63.

[12] Labillardière, *Voyage in search of La Pérouse*, 1800: 476.

[13] Duyker, *Citizen Labillardière*, 2003: 244-5.

Chapter 10: Retrospect: Recherche Bay, History and Anthropology

It must be concluded from consulting historical sources that, until recent years, the d'Entrecasteaux expedition caused few ripples in Australian historical waters. Nicolas Baudin's comparable two-vessel exploration from 1800 to 1804 fared little better, although he was fortunate to meet the Australian exploration icon, Matthew Flinders, in Encounter Bay, which helped sustain his memorable status in Australian history. D'Entrecasteaux largely sank from British public memory as Long's two lines in his *Stories of Australian exploration* (1903) bear witness: 'He cruised in Australian waters for more than a year, till he died in 1793.'[1]

Baudin benefited from a resurgence of interest as the Australian bicentennial approached. Brian Plomley set the tone in 1983 with his well-illustrated *The Baudin Expedition and the Tasmanian Aborigines*. In 1988, that superbly produced intellectual feast, *Baudin in Australian Waters*, edited by J. Bonnemains, J. Forsyth and B. Smith, brought the entire Australian collections preserved in France to public knowledge. With only seven references to the d'Entrecasteaux expedition, however, it did little to arouse awareness in Baudin's predecessor in the same Australian waters. Presumably it also was prepared for publication too early to take account of Hélène Richard's definitive *Le voyage de d'Entrecasteaux à la recherche de La Pérouse* (1986). In 1999, the Historic Houses Trust sponsored an excellent exhibition and catalogue on Baudin and Australia.[2]

Those Baudin studies evidently stimulated interest in his predecessor. Plomley and Josiane Piard-Berner edited extracts from many of the available diaries, journals and logbooks concerned with d'Entrecasteaux. Their English translation, *The General* (1993), was the first publication of much of this invaluable material as it related to Aboriginal Tasmanians. Frank Horner, who contributed a chapter to *Baudin in Australian Waters*, had already published in 1987 *The French reconnaissance: Baudin in Australia 1801-1803*. His excellently documented *Looking for La Pérouse: d'Entrecasteaux in Australia and the South Pacific 1792-1793*, followed as a sequel in 1995. Scholars are indebted to Plomley and Horner for their common sense approach.

There are several historical reasons why the results of the d'Entrecasteaux expedition (and to Tasmania particularly) featured in Australian history less than did the Baudin venture. In the first place, d'Entrecasteaux and his captains died and the voyage imploded in Java. The voluntary exile Rossel, in London until 1802, limited access to the expedition's collections. Even so, as Baudin was lavish in his praise of the quality of Beautemps-Beaupré's charts, he must have acquired copies. François Péron reflected this appreciation when he referred to the chart of Adventure Bay, 'drawn by the ingenious French artist, M. Beautemps-Beaupres [sic] is particularly to be valued, for its peculiar correctness in every detail'.[3]

Rossel's edition of d'Entrecasteaux's journal meant that the commander's *Voyage to Australia and the Pacific 1791-1793* only became available in 1808. It was a hefty two volumes, the second volume very dull from the public's viewpoint, because it comprised astronomical data and countless pages of tables. Even the first volume included Beautemps-Beaupré's invaluable, though incomprehensible to lay readers, explanation of his surveying methods. The book did not receive popular acclaim and it was 2001 before an edited English translation of most of the first volume became available. Significantly, the only translation attempted previously served technical needs. In 1823, Copeland translated Beautemps-Beaupré's account for use by naval surveyors.

Consequently, the only published source around the time when the Baudin voyage was being planned was Labillardière's *Voyage in search of La Pérouse*. It proved an international best seller in 1800, both in its French and two English versions. This indicates that public interest was sustained. By 1808, however, Trafalgar had been fought and French and British concerns lay with Napoleon and continental Europe. The British had feared French territorial ambitions in Tasmania, but that disquiet was alleviated by the fortunes of Nelson's sea warfare and by Tasmania's land settlement.

Presumably because the senior naval officers on the previous voyage were unavailable for questioning by Baudin, he must have remained largely uninformed on what they had seen and done. Labillardière was available in Paris, now a celebrity, but would a serious naval officer consult a civilian botanist? Baudin sailed from the Le Havre on 19 October 1800 and Labillardière's book had appeared by March,[4] so Baudin could read it, because copies were in the libraries on both his ships, the *Géographe* and the *Naturaliste*.[5] He would learn that Labillardière made disparaging remarks about his commander, so that was another likely reason why he should not be taken seriously.[6]

Another influential but limited circulation book became available during 1800. It was written specifically to urge Baudin to undertake serious anthropological studies — this being one of the first occasions to use the term 'anthropology'. As titled in English by its translator F. C. T. Moore in 1969, *The observation of savage peoples* set forth new ways to study societies. Its author was Joseph-Marie Degérando, who urged that 'philosophical travellers' join the expedition.

Degérando filled his 40-page memoir with remarkably 'modern' advice. He described what he termed eight faults of explorers who observed and wrote about 'savages'. These were that their accounts were incomplete and scrappy; they contained hearsay or were based on an inadequate sample; they were presented without ordering the information; they judged savages by analogies drawn from European customs; they were vaguely described; they lacked impartiality and included personal prejudices; there was a failure to learn the language; and so finally, an inability due to linguistic deficiencies to adequately present the history, traditions, beliefs of the people.[7]

He advanced a series of topics and issues an observer should record objectively. These included climate, food, the physical strength of a people, cannibalism, clothing, lifespan, intellectual qualities, concepts of human origins and ideas of existence, immortality and imagination, family life and control, kinship, role of women, modesty, social structure and relations, religious ceremonies and many other issues.[8]

This program was systematic and raised questions that became standard approaches for later social and cultural anthropologists. It anticipated handbooks such as the British Association for the Advancement of Science, *Notes and queries on anthropology for the use of travellers and residents in uncivilised lands*, (London 1874). Later editions carried less provocative titles, but *Notes and queries on anthropology* continued in service beyond the 1950s. However Degérando's schedule could be met only when an explorer mastered a language. It would be more than a century before any anthropologist spent sufficiently long periods living with a people to meet his requirements.

Degérando's stipulations resulted in the ambitious François Péron (1775–1810) accompanying the savants as a trainee zoologist, rising to the status of senior zoologist. It is evident that Degérando wrote in ignorance of Labillardière's book and Péron knew no more of d'Entrecasteaux's Tasmanian results than he scornfully read in Labillardière. Consequently, the Baudin voyage sailed to Tasmania largely in ignorance of what went before. It seems, therefore, that d'Entrecasteaux was undervalued, while credit goes to the Baudin expedition for its anthropological emphasis. Baudin's voyaging certainly achieved significant results with its scientists, which are so excellently reproduced in *Baudin in Australian Waters*. The question is, did it achieve more than its predecessor in its record of the Tasmanian people?

Plomley's verdict was that it did. 'So far as the study of man is concerned,' he wrote in 1983,

> d'Entrecasteaux's observers seemed to have made little attempt from the well tried course which had been followed by earlier expeditions, that is, they recorded what came to their notice without attempting to treat the subject as a science by posing questions and seeking answers. One of the difficulties is likely to have been that none of his scientists seem to have been particularly interested in studying man.[9]

Rhys Jones contributed an insightful essay to the Baudin corpus. Titled 'Images of natural man', it combined philosophy, history and anthropology with his Welsh fluency.[10] He examined the concepts of Rousseau and Degérando, setting Baudin's expedition into its intellectual context in order to examine Péron's work. Péron was the first field worker to employ the term 'anthropologist', although he envisaged his study of man as a branch of medical science. He employed objective tests, such as the dynamometer, which measured muscular strength, an invention of 1798.

Péron initially was influenced by Rousseau's romantic notions of Nature and the unrestricted life Man led there. In this he paralleled previous thinking. It is thought-provoking to read Rousseau on society before cultural institutions developed, where people lived in a wilderness 'whose trees were never mutilated by the axe'. Along came Labillardière to Recherche Bay, 'filled with admiration at the sight of these ancient forests, in which the sound of the axe has never been heard'. Soon after Péron landed in Tasmania, he eulogised the forest as being 'coeval with nature itself … and where the sound of the axe was never heard'.[11]

Natural man in the Tasmanian wilderness was soon demythologised by Péron and his fall from grace ushered in nineteenth century racism. His lingering romanticism was dispelled by reports of colleagues of a Western Australian woman, 'horribly ugly and disgusting. She was uncommonly lean and scraggy, and her breasts hung down almost to her thighs. The most extreme dirtiness added to her natural deformity.'[12] Tasmanian ladies were no better.[13] Those on Bruny Island were dirty and greasy, 'their shape generally lean and shrivelled, with their breasts, which were long, hanging down: in a word, all the particulars of their natural constitution were in the highest degree disgusting'. Their men were 'fierce and ferocious in their menaces, they appear at once suspicious, restless and perfidious'.[14] So violent was Péron's reaction that he undertook field tests to provide, as he believed, scientific refutation of the 'vain sophisms' of claims to noble savagery.[15]

Using the assumed objectivity of his dynamometer, in which the force of arm or leg was applied to a spring attached to a dial, he measured the strength of Tasmanians, Sydney Aborigines and Timorese. It proved to his satisfaction: 'that the inhabitants of Diemen's Land [sic], the most savage of all, and the real children of nature of the modern philosophers, are the weakest of any … Hence we may infer, that physical strength is not diminished by civilisation, nor is it a natural consequence of a savage state.'[16] As Jones concluded, Péron 'had in fact rejected the very views by which he had gained a berth on the expedition … the Aborigines of Tasmania had become symbols of his own reversal of mind'.[17]

In the light of the several d'Entrecasteaux expedition journals subsequently located and translated by Plomley, it is reasonable to question whether Plomley was premature in judging their lack of scientific attitude. Members of that expedition foreshadowed some of Degérando's research ideals. D'Entrecasteaux himself was well aware that a longer sojourn at Recherche Bay would have produced better results. Several members attempted to collect and test the accuracy of their word lists. On Bruny Island they tested their vocabulary against the Cook expedition's and found theirs to be superior. Labillardière and Delahaye provided objective comments upon the method used to throw spears. Ventenat's deductions concerning Aboriginal use of fire to hunt, and therefore to clear forest, was a remarkable conclusion. Their observations on the modesty of naked women, their collecting and cooking food, and serious attempts to observe family life, or to ascertain whether they were monogamous, approached Degérando's maxims. They virtually were a fumbling attempt at participant observation, even though they misunderstood.

More important for the fate and intellectual status of the Aboriginal Tasmanian population was the question of values. The assumed scientific approach by Péron was affected by his contempt for contemporary philosophy as typified by Rousseau. Read his final assessment of Tasmanian culture. Although it is a lengthy piece it foreshadows almost two centuries of attitudes to that society, particularly nineteenth century evolutionists.

'Without any regular chiefs,' Péron pontificated,

> without laws, or any form of government, destitute of every kind of art, having no idea of agriculture, of the use of metals, or animals; without clothing or fixed habitations, or any other retreat than a miserable penthouse [sic] of bark, to protect him against the south winds, without any arms than the tomahawk [sic] and the sogaie [spear]; always wandering in the midst of forest or on sea shores; the inhabitants of these regions unites all the characters of man in an unsocial state, and is, in every sense of the word, *the child of nature*. How different is he in his moral and physical capacities, from what is described in those seductive accounts of him by the enthusiastic imaginations of system-mongers, who have laboured to make him appear superior to man in a civilised state.[18]

It was only a short intellectual move from that analysis to the Darwinian assumptions of Edward Tylor. In 1894 he wrote a paper titled 'On the Tasmanians as representatives of Palaeolithic man,' in which he dehumanised their unchanging culture: 'just as mollusca of species first appearing far back in the earlier [geological] formations may continue to live and thrive in modern seas'.[19]

While the members of the d'Entrecasteaux team also assumed that they represented higher civilisation and sometimes expressed surprise at the level of intelligence exhibited by Tasmanians, they saw them as real humans. Nobody expressed concepts in the manner of Péron, although they judged the collection and eating of lice from the hair disgusting. While their communion with Tasmanians during that last week in 1793 reads at times like a Rousseauesque idyll, was it any less objective in its record than Péron's jaundiced version?

It must be concluded that both the d'Entrecasteaux officers and savants deserve greater credit than has been paid them. The survey and charts of Beautemps-Beaupré and Jouvency, the geomagnetic measurements by Rossel, botanical research by Labillardière and by Ventenat and Delahaye, (whose contributions may have been minimised by Labillardière) were outstanding. What may be termed the proto-anthropological and linguistic observations by several men, anticipated Baudin's achievements.

In the history of ideas, Recherche Bay contributed vitally towards fostering an intellectual approach to human society that, within its era, merits the term scientific. Above all, this was a humane and peaceful interaction. Expeditioners credited these naked and exotic people as sentient beings, not racial misfits or evolutionary survivals. These were people living in a pristine environment with strong family ties and a sense of fun. While nobody envied them their discomforts, their documentation established that the proper study of mankind is man imbued with inherent human qualities.

ENDNOTES

[1] Long, *Stories of Australian exploration*, 1903: 70.
[2] Hunt and Carter, *Terre Napoléon*, 1999.
[3] Péron, *Voyage of discovery*, 1809: 259, also 188.
[4] Duyker, *Citizen Labillardière*, 2003: 226.
[5] Cornell, *The journal of Post Captain Nicolas Baudin*, 1974: 593.
[6] See Jones, in Bonnemains, Forsyth and Smith, *Baudin in Australian waters*, 1988: 46.
[7] Degérando (ed. Moore), *The observation of savage peoples*, 1969: 65-9.
[8] Degérando (ed. Moore), *The observation of savage peoples*, 1969: 70-104.
[9] Plomley, *The Baudin expedition*, 1983: 9.
[10] Jones, in Bonnemains, Forsyth and Smith, *Baudin in Australian waters*, 1988: 35-64.
[11] Jones, in Bonnemains, Forsyth and Smith, *Baudin in Australian waters*, 1988: 35 – Rousseau; Labillardière, *Voyage in search of La Pérouse*, 1800: 94 – Labillardière; Jones, in Bonnemains, Forsyth and Smith, *Baudin in Australian waters*, 1988: 44, quotes Péron.
[12] Péron, *Voyage of discovery*, 1809: 67-8.
[13] Ibid.: 197.
[14] Ibid.: 217.
[15] Ibid.: 186.
[16] Ibid.: 313-14.
[17] Jones, in Bonnemains, Forsyth and Smith, *Baudin in Australian waters*, 1988: 46.
[18] Péron, *Voyage of discovery*, 1809: 313.
[19] Tylor, *Journal Anthropological Institute* 22 (1894): 141-52; quotation 150.

Chapter 11: The Chaotic Years

While the spectacular environs of Recherche Bay conceal secrets of pre-European Tasmanian existence and symbolise their sociable racial interaction with the first European visitors, its significance does not end in 1793. Across the past two centuries the history and archaeology of this remote place comprises a palimpsest of diverse European endeavours. Developing and decaying as they did, such pioneering industrial initiatives and associated social conditions provide thought-provoking testimony and material traces for all Australians. This constitutes a truly cultural landscape of national status to cherish and preserve. It offers a rich resource for cultural tourism that could sustain an industry other than forestry, with mutual benefits to employment and heritage.

Whaling

In 1804, the year that David Collins established the Risdon Cove settlement, an English whaler already was exploiting the whaling prospects of Adventure Bay. Two years later, William Collins established a bay whaling post at Ralphs Bay on the Derwent estuary. Over the following three decades, eastern Tasmania and Bass Strait became a global centre for whaling and sealing.[1] Sadly, the region witnessed the introduction of destructive diseases into the Aboriginal population and the abduction of females, well ahead of the tide of Tasmanian land settlement.

George Augustus Robinson has relevant information about the impact of whalers or sealers on the Aboriginal population. He talked with a girl whose hands and feet had been tied when she was placed in a boat and taken away. She claimed that there were 50 such women then in Bass Strait. More specifically, he reported that there were three Bruny Island women who had been abducted.[2] Diseases invaded men, women and children, to add to the demographic impact of the abductions. In 1829, Robinson reported the deaths of 10 persons, eight from Bruny Island and two from Port Davey. Most illnesses originated with colds. A few days later, the total of dead reached 22. By February 1831, he believed that, throughout south-east Tasmania, including Recherche Bay and Bruny, only several people had survived.[3]

The shore-based whaling industry, which saw bay whalers working at Recherche Bay by the 1820s, was a dangerous, bloody and short-lived industry. It was encouraged by a reduction in the English duty on whale oil in 1828.[4] Crews harvested the southern right (or 'black') whales, *Eubalaena australis*, as they migrated up the D'Entrecasteaux Channel from the Antarctic during the winter. Pregnant females sought calm harbour waters in which to calve, so Recherche Bay was a superior haven as its waters were the required minimum of five metres deep. They fell easy prey to hunters, but proved an obviously non-renewable resource as pregnant females were the prime target. The Bay offered another natural advantage for whalers, in that the Actaeon Reef outside the harbour entrance assisted the hunt by blocking an exit for escaping harpooned whales. George Augustus Robinson was present there in 1833 and described the reef's value and the dangers of the trade. He was told that during the 1832 winter season around 100 whales were slaughtered there.[5] As this was an average of at least two whales a day, the waters must have been turbulent and bloodied with thrashing bodies. During 1839 more than 1,000 right whales were harpooned in Tasmanian waters; 645 whales died in 1837, resulting in a financial return of £135,210.[6] The oil and baleen bone were sought eagerly in London for lighting, cooking and corsets, amongst other uses. This ruthless industry was self-destructive. By the 1840s the stream of right whales diminished and deep-ocean whaling of other species was substituted. A shore-based station persisted at Recherche Bay for another 20 years, but returns were small.

Imlay shore-based whaling station, 2006. John Mulvaney

The Imlay shore-based whaling station at Snake Point. Whale carcasses were winched onto this sloping rock for flensing. Photograph by John Mulvaney, 2006.

In his careful archaeological survey around Recherche Bay, Parry Kostoglou located 15 separate sites, six on Gagen's Point, where the evidence revealed occupation traces — basal remnants of huts or stores, glass and ceramics, chimney butts and whalebone.[7] Life for the whalers during their winter vigil must have been rudimentary and cold in their bark huts. Robinson arrived there in March 1833, before the main whaling season, but found 'the shore is strewed with putrid carcasses and bones ... There are still remaining on shore numerous huts and iron pots where they boil down, or try, the oil.'[8]

Robinson was on Bruny Island during the 1829 winter. He described a whale hunt involving seven boats, each crewed with six oarsmen and a cox-harpoonist.[9] Such figures imply that 49 men were involved in competitive killing of one whale. By 1836, at least 260 men were employed in the industry.[10]

Fisher Point pilot station and pub, 2006. John Mulvaney

The Fisher Point pilot station, established in 1836 and abandoned 1851, when whaling virtually ceased. Subsequently it became a rowdy pub frequented by deep-sea whalers. Photograph by John Mulvaney, 2006

With so many ships entering the harbour, in 1836 a pilot's station was established on the southern headland (Fisher's Point), given a permanent presence for a few years, until it was abandoned in 1851.[11] Recherche Bay must have been a competitive and potentially unruly place as whaling teams sought the same quarry from co-existing shore stations. The pilot station became a pub, which attracted crews of deep-sea whalers. The boisterous Sawyers Arms quenched deep thirsts.

That boundary disputes existed both on land concerning space to process the whale and on sea as to which team harpooned first, is understandable. For example, at Cockle Creek during the 1830s there were four whaling stations. In 1833, the government intervened. The Colonial Surveyor, J. E. Calder, arrived to delimit boundaries between leases allotted to the rival parties. Even when the industry was in decline, the Crown issued seven leases for bay whaling stations at Recherche Bay between 1840 and 1859. Surviving archaeological sites are valuable testimony to the harsh way of life involved in Tasmania's first major export industry. Recherche Bay played a prominent role in that primitive economy.

The dolerite rocks defining the bay in places provided sloping flat platforms for some shore-based whale fisheries to flense a whale carcase. One is on Gagen's Point, but the most striking facility is at Snake Point, near Fisher's Point. It was capable of holding a carcase once it was winched from the sea. Traces of bricks and other relics occur in the wooded area behind this massive rock, evidence for the crude shelters in which men sheltered. This station was established in 1835 by Alexander Imlay.

Symbolising the dangers of this violent profession is the nearby gravestone of Samuel Thomas Pryat. He died aboard the *Alladin*, off Southwest Cape, aged in his 20s, a possible shipmate of the ill-fated Aboriginal man William Lanney. Lady Jane Franklin's visit to the bay in 1838 provided testimony to the busy and smelly harbour. On Gagen's Point she observed Kerr's whaling station equipped with shear-legs for carving up a carcase.

Piracy on the Brig *Cyprus*

During August 1829, Recherche Bay was the venue for an act of piracy. It had repercussions in several lands, resulting in three men being hanged, but the ringleader escaped with his life. The deed was celebrated in a well-known ballad and, it is claimed, in London's theatreland. It was the subject of a book by Frank Clune and Inky Stevenson in 1962. A good yarn, it is entirely undocumented, although it appears to quote many sources.[12]

The two-masted brig *Cyprus*, 108 tons, measured 24 metres by six, so it was overcrowded with 64 persons aboard. It was transporting 33 hardened convicts in irons from Hobart to the west coast penal establishment at Macquarie Harbour. Also on board were Lieutenant Carew and a dozen 63rd Regiment soldiers transferred to its garrison. Carew's wife and two children and the wife and child of a soldier added to the crowded conditions. Fortunately for the mutineers, the ship carried three months worth of stores for the penal settlement on Sarah Island.

The vessel became stormbound for a week in Recherche Bay, time for the convicts to hatch an escape plot. Carew was a new chum and an irresolute character who was lulled into a false sense of trust by the deliberate good behaviour of the convicts. To relieve the boredom and fetid atmosphere of their cramped quarters, Carew charitably allowed five convicts at a time to exercise on deck, minus their chains. He and the doctor went fishing, possibly lured off the ship by convict John Popjoy (or Pobjoy) who requested an urgent hearing out of earshot of his fellow prisoners. At least he was in their boat, leaving four unchained convicts taking exercise on deck.

Security was lax, with only two armed guards, the other soldiers were lazing below deck. They were easily overcome by the convicts and a chicken coop was placed over the hatchway preventing the soldiers from climbing the ladder. Shots were fired harmlessly up through the deck, but the troops were silenced with boiling water down the hatch. Within minutes the ship was captured and all prisoners unchained. Carew was not allowed aboard and, fearing for his family, obeyed orders to go ashore. After five trips in the rowing boat, all the civilians, sailors and convicts who rejected the choice of sailing free, were dumped ashore. Minimal food and clothing accompanied them. Late that day Popjoy deserted the mutineers and swam ashore.

Woodcut of *Cyprus* castaways attributed to W. B. Gould, 1829. Archives Office of Tasmania

William Buelow Gould probably sketched 'the making of the coracle', a woodcut in *The Hobart Town Courier*, 12 September 1829. It depicts the *Cyprus* castaways. Convicts are assisted by Mrs Carew while Lieut. Carew despairs, head in hands. Archives Office of Tasmania

Except that the two guards had sore heads, nobody was injured and the incident was carried out without fuss. The vessel sailed away with 18 men, navigated by a former seaman answering to the name William Swallow and many other aliases. In a remarkable feat of navigation, with a crew unused to manning a vessel, they sailed the Pacific with only one casualty, the loss of a man overboard when aloft at the sails. They touched at New Zealand, by-passed Tahiti because of unfavourable winds, spent six weeks at Niuatoputapu (Keppel's Island), where seven men chose to remain. The remaining 10 crew sailed on across the Pacific.

Swallow claimed that they reached Japan, where they were fired upon. In a recent detailed evaluation David Sissons demonstrated that this was one of Swallow's ingenious fabrications. They never reached Japan, but did reach the Chinese coast. Voluntarily leaving two men at an island en route and another man subsequently, they headed for Whampoa (the outer part of Canton). They scuttled the *Cyprus* when near China and rowed off in the ship's boat, now renamed *Edward*, with a false story to match that they were distressed sailors from that ship. It was then February 1830.[13]

Those 44 people marooned on the beach at Recherche Bay included 15 'trusty' convicts. Popjoy was one of them, having deserted the pirates that night by diving overboard and swimming ashore. Lieutenant Carew was totally unprepared to lead this dispirited group and initiatives came chiefly from the convicts. Brush and bark shelters were erected and two convicts departed to walk to Hobart, one of them the ubiquitous Popjoy. They swam across the Huon River, but claimed that they were threatened by Aborigines and swam back to safety across the river leaving their clothes behind. They returned naked and scratched to the dejected party. Five convicts then volunteered to reach Hobart via an inland route, so avoiding broad river mouths, but they failed to reach Hobart before they were rescued in poor condition. One of these convicts was William Buelow Gould, an artist who was destined to gain local celebrity as an artist and drunkard. Subsequently he prepared an etching for the *Hobart Town Courier*. It depicts Welsh sailor Morgan making the coracle, with Lieutenant Carew sitting on a rock, hands over his face in despair, while his wife assists with the coracle. 170 years later, Gould gained greater fictional celebrity in *Gould's book of fish* by writer Richard Flanagan.[14] Popjoy is prominent in Flanagan's saga, but the *Cyprus* incident escapes mention.

Morgan ingeniously constructed the coracle using a knife, a razor and canvas across pliable wattle sticks. It was waterproofed with beeswax and soap from personal kits. Remarkably, it proved seaworthy and Morgan and Popjoy set forth using rough-hewn paddles. They only needed to cross the D'Entrecasteaux Channel to Partridge Island, fortunately in calm waters, to seek assistance from the *Orelia*. That vessel sent a relief boat to the rescue, while another was sent to Hobart with Morgan and Popjoy.

The news created great excitement and the Hobart press made much of the garbled news. The castaways were rescued, Lieutenant Carew was court-martialled but exonerated, and Popjoy became a public hero. His reward was a full pardon, so he soon sailed for London.[15]

When George Augustus Robinson sailed into Recherche Bay on 1 February 1830, the brush shelters were still there.[16] Their location offers an attractive archaeological puzzle. Where were they camping during the 10 days before their rescue? There may exist archaeological traces of their stay. The fact that the

Cyprus sheltered for a week, moored sufficiently close to shore for Popjoy to swim, might favour a location on the north-eastern peninsula beach, scene of the 1792 French visit. But Lady Jane Franklin's comments in 1838 are relevant. She wrote of the northern sector of the western side of the harbour as the site of the castaways. Then she had second thoughts and added a note: 'On reconsideration, I believe the landing place in question was the W point of the most western of the coves which I have called Lucas Cove.'[17] That would be in the Rocky Bay area, possibly in Coalbins Bay or Mottes Beach.

Robinson, who was travelling with Bruny Island people who were witnesses, told of a terrible deed carried out by the pirates before they sailed. Provided that his evidence is accepted and that the crew concerned was on the *Cyprus*, Robinson accused the crew of abducting the wife of his Aboriginal friend, Mangana. This consigned her to what may be described as a fate worse than death. No other sources refer to this kidnapping, although Robinson evidently made an official report on this event.[18]

Popjoy and the pirates were destined to collide in London, resulting in Popjoy becoming a veritable killjoy. The seven men from the *Edward* duly presented themselves to British authorities in Canton, where their story of shipwreck was accepted. Four of them including Swallow (now Captain Waldron) signed on as crew on *Charles Grant* for London. The remaining three sailed for America and fortunate obscurity on the Danish barque *Pulen*. The *Charles Grant* arrived in London on 7 September, the convicts having foolishly sold items from the *Cyprus* to fellow crew members, later to incriminate them.

They were unaware that on 1 September the *Kellie Castle* arrived fom Canton, having outsailed their ship, with news of their true identity. The three convicts who had left the *Cyprus* near China also turned up in the Canton area and two of them told contradictory versions; George Davis even forgot the agreed name of his captain! Then the Sydney newspapers arrived with the Recherche Bay story and one of the convicts confessed. The *Kellie Castle* sailed to bring the news to England, with Davis as a prisoner. When the convicts disembarked from the *Charles Grant*, they were arrested, except for Swallow who disappeared for a time, until captured.

It was at their trial that their nemesis, Popjoy, intervened to provide testimony, rather selectively, against the men. He had arrived legitimately in London as a free man during July 1830. He had worked his passage home on a ship, in which a passenger was Hobart prison's head gaoler. He had voyaged to London for the trial of another celebrated convict, Ikey Solomon, who Charles Dickens transformed into Fagan. Consequently, fate produced two men willing to identify the prisoners. Swallow ingeniously told long and involved tales of how the convicts had forced him to navigate the ship, while he took no part in the initial piracy. He convinced the jury, which found him, the ringleader, not guilty.

'The axe had never sounded'

Two men, Davis and Watt were hanged at Execution Dock, over a century since Captain Kidd's execution there for piracy. Possibly these unfortunates were the last men to be executed in England for piracy. Another convict, James Camm, subsequently arrested in the Pacific, was hanged at Hobart.[19]

Swallow had committed a serious offence by returning to England, made worse by thefts committed following his return. So he and the other two convicts were sentenced for life and transported back to Hobart. They arrived at Macquarie Harbour prison two years later than the law had intended.

Robinson almost certainly talked with Swallow there in 1833.[20] Robinson thought him 'in a dying state'. In fact he died at Port Arthur a year later. A con man with forethought and vivid imagination, he was sole navigator of the *Cyprus* around the greater Pacific. He merited fully the praises sung by Frank the Poet in the following ballad, still popular after more than 150 years.

> Come all you sons of Freedom, a chorus join with me,
> I'll sing a song of heros, and glorious liberty.
> Some lads condemn'd from England sail'd to Van Dieman's Shore,
> Their Country, friends and parents, perhaps never to see more.
> When landed in this colony to different Masters went,
> For trifling offences, t'Hobart Town gaol were sent,
> A second sentence being incurr'd we were order'd for to be
> Sent to Macquarie Harbour, that place of tyranny.
> The hardships we'd to undergo, are matters of record,
> But who believes the convict, or who regards his word?
> For starv'd and flogg'd and punish'd, deprived of all redress,
> The Bush our only refuge, with death to end distress.
> Hundreds of us were shot down, for daring to be free,
> Numbers caught and banished, to life-long slavery.
>
> Brave Swallow, Watt and Davis, were in our noble band
> Determin'd at the first slant, to quit Van Dieman's Land.
> March'd down in chains and guarded, on the CYPRUS BRIG convey'd
> The topsails being hoisted, the anchor being weighed.
> The wind it blew Sou'Sou'West and on we went straightaway,
> Till we found ourselves wind-bound, in gloomy Recherche Bay.
> 'Twas August eighteen twenty nine, with thirty one on board,
> Lieutenant Carew left the Brig, and soon we passed the word
> The Doctor too was absent, the soldiers off their guard,
> A better opportunity could never have occur'd.
> Confin'd within a dismal hole, we soon contriv'd a plan,
> To capture now the CYPRUS, or perish every man.
> But thirteen turn'd faint-hearted and begg'd to go ashore,
> So eighteen boys rush'd daring, and took the Brig and store.

> We first address'd the soldiers "for liberty we crave,
> Give up your arms this instant, or the sea will be your grave,
> By tyranny we've been oppress'd, by your Colonial laws,
> But we'll bid adieu to slavery, or die in freedom's cause."
> We next drove off the Skipper, who came to help his crew,
> Then gave three cheers for liberty, 'twas answer'd cheerly too.
> We brought the sailors from below, and row'd them to the land
> Likewise the wife and children of Carew in command.
> Supplies of food and water, we gave the vanquish'd crew,
> Returning good for evil, as we'd been taught to do.
> We mounted guard with Watch and Ward, then haul'd the boat aboard,
> We elected William Swallow, and obey'd our Captain's word.
> The Morn broke bright the Wind was fair, we headed for the sea
> With one more cheer for those on shore and glorious liberty.
> For Navigating smartly Bill Swallow was the man,
> Who laid a course out neatly to take us to Japan.
> Then sound your golden trumpets, play on your tuneful notes,
> The CYPRUS BRIG is sailing, how proudly now she floats.
> May fortune help th'Noble lads, and keep them ever free
> From Gags, and Cats, and Chains, and Traps, and Cruel Tyranny.[21]

ENDNOTES

[1] Information on Tasmanian whaling comes from the carefully researched unpublished report to the Parks and Wildlife Service by Kathryn Evans, 1993; see also Nash, *The bay whalers*, 2003.

[2] Plomley (ed.), *Friendly mission*, 1966: 32.

[3] Ibid.: 76, 226 n35.

[4] Robson, *History of Tasmania*, 1983: 261.

[5] Plomley (ed.), *Friendly mission*, 1966: 710.

[6] Evans, 'Shore-based whaling in Tasmania', vol. 1: 23; Woolley and Smith, *A history of the Huon*, 2004: 160.

[7] Kostoglou's systematic survey is summarised by Evans, 'Shore-based whaling in Tasmania', vol. 2: 20-3; Nash, *The bay whalers*, 2003.

[8] Plomley (ed.), *Friendly mission*, 1966: 709.

[9] Ibid.: 71.

[10] Evans, 'Shore-based whaling in Tasmania', vol. 1, p. 22.

[11] Woolley and Smith, *A history of the Huon*, 2004: 123, 210 n707.

[12] There are numerous references to the *Cyprus* affair, many of them garbled. The most detailed version is by Clune and Stevenson, *The pirates of the Brig Cyprus*, 1962. It combines detailed conversations between the pirates, highly fictional, with evident quotations from anonymous but official London documents. What trust can the reader place in such undocumented 'faction'? For London theatre performance, John West, *History of Tasmania*, 1852, vol 2: 215; Ingleton, *True patriots all*, 1952: 129 – for the ballad.

[13] This account is only as reliable as Clune and Stevenson. A detailed examination of the *Cyprus* in the Pacific was written by the late David Sissons, forthcoming in the *Journal of Pacific History*. It corrects many errors.

[14] Flanagan, *Gould's book of fish*, 2001.

[15] The best contemporary version is in Hobart's *Colonial Times*, 28 August, 4 September 1829. See also Lemprière (1839). There is new information in Pretyman, *Papers and Proceedings Royal Society of Tasmania* 88 (1954).

[16] Plomley (ed.), *Friendly mission*, 1966: 113.

[17] Mackaness, *Correspondence of Sir John and Lady Jane Franklin*, 1947: 44.

[18] Plomley (ed.), *Friendly mission*, 1966: 75-6. Clune and Stevenson, *The pirates of the Brig Cyprus*, 1962: 84-5, doubt whether those responsible were on the *Cyprus*, but appear to quote official documents which identify the action with *Cyprus*.

[19] The above account drew upon Clune and Stevenson who quote what must be trial documents.

[20] Plomley (ed.), *Friendly mission*, 1966: 732, 30 May 1833.

[21] Quoted in Ingleton, *True patriots all*, 1952: 129. Ingleton, p. 289, identifies Frank the Poet as Frank Macnamara, who died in 1852.

Chapter 12: Lady Jane at Recherche Bay

Lady Jane Franklin was one of Australia's most enterprising wives of colonial governors. She was energetic, incurably inquisitive and had faith in improving people through industry and education. In 1838 she purchased 1280 acres of virgin forestland on the western bank of the Huon River, naming it Huon Fernlands (Franklin today). Her vision was to convert it into a settlement of free tenant farmers who would strive to purchase the land. Sea and river transport were essential to supply the settlers, so she arranged for a boat to be constructed for £300. It was built at Port Davey from Huon pine. Named *Huon Pine*, it was completed in 1839.

Late in 1838, the Franklins hosted a visit from the ornithologist John Gould and his artist wife. Captain King, the superintendent of government vessels, wanted to assess Huon pine resources, so Lady Jane seized the opportunity to accompany him to inspect her *Huon Pine* at Port Davey. Joining the party on the government schooner were six passengers, including Lady Jane, John Gould and Ronald Campbell Gunn, public servant, advisor to the governor and a botanist of note. Five accompanying servants ensured they spent a pleasant voyage. To guide the vessel, Bruce, the Recherche Bay pilot, was recommended but they preferred an elderly retired pilot, Lucas.[1]

Bad weather drove them to shelter in Recherche Bay for about one week. Although Lady Jane suffered from toothache, even the bad weather did not prevent her from exploring. First, she was rowed to the D'Entrecasteaux River. She then turned her attention to the French visit and the garden. Lucas, the pilot, 'knew nothing of the garden,' but he remembered two trees fallen onto the beach, to which inscribed copper plates had been nailed. When he saw them years before an inscription still survived. They followed a track through the bush made by whalers, then walked along the sandy beach until they reached the trees. The inscription had disappeared, but rusty nails which had fixed the notice attracted Lady Jane's interest, so she souvenired one of them and one of 'two circular knobs' carved near the base of the trunk. Could this have been a remnant of the carving of Wraeggowraper, referred to by Robinson?[2] At least one inscription left by the French, according to the log of *l'Espérance*, was the latitude and longitude.[3]

They probably were close to Delahaye's garden at this time. Some days later when they again searched for the garden, they were in the wrong area, evidently too far north, so they failed to locate it, although they may have found another

French attempt at gardening.[4] The only source for her knowledge of the garden must have been Labillardière. Gunn made a further unsuccessful search.

Lady Jane's diary contains clues to the busy waters of D'Entrecasteaux Channel and of human activities within the bay. During those few days she mentions a whaleboat, a barque from England and two vessels en route to Hobart, a schooner for the same destination, a storeship for the pilot station and the Bruny Island lighthouse and a ship bound for London. Within the harbour was a whaling station, with shears erected for cutting up the carcase. A boat had collected a load of whale oil. Not surprisingly, and in the best Victorian prose, she complained that 'our olfactory nerves were sorely disturbed by the effluvia from some putrid whale carcases which were lying on the sand'. She trusted that whaling days would have ended before the proposed Ramsgate settlement below Catamaran River built 'its lodging houses and bathing machines'.[5] That proposed settlement never eventuated, although the place was surveyed.

While Gould collected bird nests and eggs with persistence, even visiting an island in the Channel and capturing a live penguin, Gunn and Lady Jane were interested in the economic prospects for coal mining. Gunn observed the coal seams in the Cockle Creek area reported by Labillardière, but considered that the coal was of a 'very indifferent kind,' so another 60 years passed before a serious attempt was made to exploit coal in that area.

Exploring the area near the French garden indicated on the map, they came upon traces of coal. This time, a sample was collected and sent to Hobart.[6] Although it was 1840 before any commercial interest, this action signified the beginning of a brief coal mining enterprise on the north-eastern peninsula.

Despite toothache, bad weather and the pervading stench, Lady Jane enjoyed herself. She even assigned place names (Mount King, Lucas Bay) in the approved imperial manner, despite the likelihood that they had European names already. Finally, praise for the coastal surveying by the d'Entrecasteaux expedition: it 'laid them down with an accuracy which leaves nothing more to be desired'.[7]

These few observant days at Recherche Bay provide a valuable record, and stimulated an interest in coal. They are an interesting social document on life on the pioneering frontier. Their presence at Recherche Bay links the names of prominent Victorian individuals — Lady Jane Franklin, John Gould and R. C. Gunn — with this cultural landscape.

It was 1840 before Hobart business interests took the presence of coal seriously. Hobart was supplied with coal from the convict-mined Saltwater River mine on Tasman Peninsula. This Recherche Bay coal was said to be superior to the latter, so a company was formed and an exploratory shaft was sunk. To critics it seemed a cosy arrangement, where investors were supplied with free convict labour, working in competition with the government colliery's convict workforce on the Tasman Peninsula. Initially the coal was found to be of good quality, although this decreased with time as much sediment was mixed with it. Around 1,300 tons were shipped to Hobart but the area was soon exhausted, despite the investment in sinking two shafts. The main shaft, a circular masonry-lined hole, reached a depth of 36 metres. However, most of the coal was won from the beachside outcrop rather than from underground. Traces of this work still exist on and near the beach adjacent to the 'French garden'. During the years 1841–2 the flow of coal to Hobart was small. 1843 was the peak production year, when 70 convicts laboured there. Critics drew attention to the fact that most labourers had been transferred from the government colliery at Saltwater River, consequently decreasing its output.

The end of the Van Diemen's Land Coal Company approached. Two workmen admitted to the Hobart hospital suffered from advanced scurvy. Clearly the company underfed and exploited its labour force, and the Colonial Secretary demanded the attendance at the mine of a doctor. Such costs were beyond the company's resources, so the short-lived company collapsed. The initial coal mining enterprise at Recherche Bay lasted only about three years.[8]

Recherche Bay illustrates the problem of finding a staple industry that could sustain permanent settlement. Whaling and coal mining proved to be non-renewable resources. The pilot's station established in 1836 was withdrawn in 1851.[9] Timber was an obvious candidate for that staple. Back in 1833 Robinson observed gangs of timber workers 'sawing timber for different persons'.[10] It is not known whether this temporary activity produced timber for local use by whalers, or whether it was shipped to Hobart.

There was a brief revival in timber getting at Recherche Bay during the years 1853–4. This was a direct consequence of the Victorian gold rush, when suddenly increased population required housing. It is said that hundreds of timber workers came to Recherche Bay. In 1854 a steam-powered mill was established on the western side, at Waterhole cove, where d'Entrecasteaux obtained water. Some pubs were associated with this thirsty industry, but the patrons presumably left the area because the *Sawyers Arms* licence was not renewed following 1854.[11]

With sawn timber available, there were opportunities to build or repair boats. The 1863 survey map shows three huts at Bennetts (Observatory) Point, with a sailing boat, labeled 'craft' on the land. It is situated in the area where the large artificial rock platform stands today which may have served the builders. At least two boats were built at Recherche Bay in 1853–4, presumably at the place indicated on the map. A 22-ton cutter, *Recherche*, was built in 1853 and the 58-ton schooner, *Friends*, was constructed in 1854.[12] Possibly this dry-stone platform was first constructed in 1792 and enlarged during the 1850s.

One of the ship builders was Thomas Moreland, who had a whaling station at Gagen's Point for some years. In 1855 he applied to purchase 10 acres there, presumably the location of the district's first post office, as Moreland was appointed postmaster. Around the same period, Richard Woolley obtained land near the former pilot station.[13] During the mid-1850s, therefore, some permanent settlers were adjusting to life there. Around 1833, at the height of the whaling boom, a surveyed township area had been laid out between Cockle Creek and Catamaran River. It was named Ramsgate, but it was 20 years before people decided for a permanent existence at Recherche Bay, and even then, the numbers proved ephemeral.

ENDNOTES

[1] Based upon Mackaness, *Correspondence of Sir John and Lady Jane Franklin*, 1947: 38-9; Woolley and Smith, *A history of the Huon*, 2004: 75.

[2] Mackaness, *Correspondence of Sir John and Lady Jane Franklin*, 1947: 43; Plomley (ed.), *Friendly mission*, 1966: 376.

[3] Plomley and Piard-Bernier, *The General*, 1993: 75.

[4] Mackaness, *Correspondence of Sir John and Lady Jane Franklin*, 1947: 48, 50.

[5] Ibid.: 43.

[6] Ibid.: 42, 49-50.

[7] Ibid.: 53.

[8] Information drawn from Woolley and Smith, *A history of the Huon*, 2004: 163-8.

[9] Woolley and Smith, *A history of the Huon*, 2004: 123, 210 n707.

[10] Plomley (ed.), *Friendly mission*, 1966: 709.

[11] Woolley and Smith, *A history of the Huon*, 2004: 123-4, 147.

[12] Woolley and Smith, *A history of the Huon*, 2004: 153; District Surveyor, G. Innes map, dated November 1863, County of Kent, Parish of Purves.

[13] Woolley and Smith, *A history of the Huon*, 2004: 123.

Chapter 13: Good and Bad Times

A thriving sawmilling industry existed at two centres around the bay by 1900. The steam-driven mill continued at Waterhole Cove until 1868. Then the industry faltered until 1884, when large sawmills were established by the Catamaran River and at Leprena on the western side of the northern bay. By 1900 the population living there exceeded 100 at each centre. It was around the turn of the century that coal mining also offered employment, and an active industrial period followed for a few years. The seams of coal proved limited or uneconomic. As trees were felled, their distance from the sawmill increased. This required timber rail tramways establishing a network radiating out from an area and moved on when that area was harvested. The same applied to transporting coal.

By 1939 a complex network radiated from harbour-based centres at Catamaran, Leprena and Cockle Creek. Traces of these lines survive today in regrowth forests.[1] One moss-covered segment runs by the shore on the north-eastern peninsula in the area of the French activities in 1792.

The timber industry is necessarily situated in forests, so bushfires prove a recurring hazard. The Catamaran mill was destroyed in a 1914 bushfire, coinciding with the abandonment of the coal mine there. The spasmodic and transitory nature of frontier employment was again demonstrated at Recherche Bay when the community of around 100 people, supporting a school and a store, faced sudden unemployment. Today the media feature factory closures and speculate about the future employment of the urban employees. The history of much of rural Australia also has been a boom and bust story of employment, as rural industries prosper then fold. Recherche Bay is a classic example. On a smaller scale than urban plant closures, the impact upon the families dependant upon a timber mill or colliery was no less drastic.

Some people moved away to seek employment, a solution easily but drastically met in 1939 with the outbreak of war. Others chose to remain as self-sufficient food producers. The trade-off was the fresh air, scenery and freedom. The soil suited vegetables and small market gardens sustained a few people, with cabbage growing a feature. Flower gardens remain prominent in memories, indicating that, even in stressful situations, people have values beyond economic survival. In the meantime garden produce, hunting and the resources of the harbour sustained those who remained behind awaiting the next outbreak of industrial activity.

'The axe had never sounded'

Machinery at Leprena mill site, 2006. John Mulvaney

A power source, a boiler for Leprena mill, now lost in the bush. Photograph by John Mulvaney, 2006

Further north, the Leprena sawmill complex continued to expand until 1939, when that enterprise also closed. Another 100 or so people who had congregated there faced a similar choice of whether to leave or subsist. At its peak, the mill supplied workers with bread; the bakery oven survives as a ruin amidst forest.

During the 1920s the Leprena sawmill produced up to 50,000 super feet per week. The logs arrived on trollies that ran on the wooden tramlines. All the logs were cut from a selected area and within a practical haulage radius. When that area was cleared of suitable trees, the tramlines were extended to exploit a new forested sector. In laying down the rails it was essential to consider the gradient that the steam engine hauling the logs could negotiate. As the mill needed to keep working, the axemen were assigned a daily number of wagon-loads of saw logs. Lighters transported the sawn timber to Bennetts Point, where it was loaded onto a ship.[2] The extensive wharf at Leprena suvives today as hundreds of timber decking planks in the mud and substantial posts.

Parry Kostoglou made an exhaustive archaeological survey of the remains of the Recherche Bay timber industry, which effectively ended in 1939 with the closure of the Leprena sawmill. Smaller operations cut out remaining stands of old growth trees and regrowth timber during the 1930s and 1940s. Since then, the forest has regrown, so that today the French explorers would find the view in some directions not unlike the romantic scenery which inspired them.

Leprena timber mill site, 2006. John Mulvaney

The Leprena timber mill wharf in 2006, last used around 1940. Photograph by John Mulvaney

Kostoglou's research indicates that seven large sawmill enterprises operated sporadically at Recherche Bay between 1884 and 1952, while perhaps six small sawmills intermittently exploited the bay's resources between 1897 and 1957. Significantly, if the development of a systematic ecotourism industry was contemplated, the surviving remains are extensive. Omitting the many northern identified places on the Lune River and Southport Lagoon, the number of archaeological sites identified by Kostoglou between the D'Entrecasteaux River area and Cockle Creek is 36. These include mill sites, sawdust heaps, discarded machinery, tramways, wharves and house areas. The tidal and waterlogged zone around Leprena has preserved considerable areas of tramway and the traces of the wharf extend for 300 metres. This complex represents an industrial heritage worth preserving for potential ecotourism that also stresses archaeology.[3] Kostoglou's perceptive consultancy report merits publication, with its memorable photographic documentation. It demonstrates the rapidity of environmental change in a wet, forested environment.

'The axe had never sounded'

Timber mill remains, Cockle Creek, 2006. John Mulvaney

Remains of the timber mill at Cockle Creek, one of the last mills around the bay. Photograph by John Mulvaney, 2006

Coal Mining

The coal industry was subject to comparable fluctuating fortunes. Presumably, early timber getters for the Catamaran mill must have seen coal exposed at the surface from uprooted trees. It is no coincidence, therefore, that the first coal mining attempts were in that area around 1900. Prospects were judged sufficient in 1902 to attract the Minister of Mines and the Government Geologist, W. H. Twelvetrees, on a tour of inspection.[4] They also visited the Glen colliery, south of Leprena, where coal was found in 1899. On this latter prospect, Twelvetrees was non-committal in his report, observing 'nothing much can be said beyond that coal seams undoubtedly exist'.[5] And nothing much did eventuate there.

Twelvetrees recommended boring at some locations in the Mesozoic sandstone on the prospective Catamaran and Glen fields. His map shows that an extensive timber tramway already linked the mine with Catamaran River mouth. This tramway was sufficiently stable to bear the weight of 12-ton logs, so he presumably thought that it might also serve the coal industry.

A sample of coal collected by Twelvetrees from the existing six-metre shaft proved capable of powering the steamer upon which he sailed. Significantly, however, the shaft had to be baled out and water level was a constant problem. Twelvetrees noted another limiting factor due to water was that the coal tended to be friable ('to make slack') and break up into small pieces, which could choke a furnace. This placed severe limitations on saleability. Following this visit, the Catamaran Coal Mining Company produced coal until 1906, when its capital ran out.[6] Undercapitalisation was a permanent feature of the various company attempts to mine.

Between 1907 and 1921 abortive and costly attempts were made to mine the coal at Catamaran, boosted by a cursory but grandiose report in 1912 which predicted over two million tons of coal from the 317 acre lease. A wharf and large coal bins were constructed, only to be destroyed later by fire, and over two kilometres of steel tramway was laid down along the former wooden tramway's route. The scheme's finances collapsed. When the tunnel collapsed a later project failed.

Work commenced in 1914 to sink a 40 metre deep shaft to access a three metre thick coal seam. Funding ran out as usual, and that shaft entrance is visible today over a kilometre north-west of the Catamaran bridge. Indeed, the entire coal mining area, now largely revegetated, contains many hidden hazards for unwary bush walkers.

Base of coal storage bin, Evoralls Point, 2006. John Mulvaney

Concrete base of the coal bin and loader at Evoralls Point. Photograph by John Mulvaney, 2006

That new main shaft was pumped out in 1923 when mining recommenced and major works became possible in 1925 through new investment. A narrow gauge tramline over three kilometres long was constructed to the deep water at Evoralls Point, where facilities for storage of 1,200 tons and rapid loading were provided.

The *James Craig* was purchased for use as a coal hulk, to be towed to Hobart when filled. Substantial concrete foundations on the high land at Evoralls Point, surviving today, indicate where the coal was conveyed down to sea level. They are overgrown with trees and understorey, as are the traces of the tramway. 75 years sufficed to convert a very visible industrial complex to archaeological remnants.

Overturned tram engine near Evoralls Point, 2006. John Mulvaney

Overturned tram engine on tramway to Evoralls Point coal bin. Photograph by John Mulvaney, 2006

This time production appeared to justify the expenditure, when 9,950 tons of coal were produced during 1926 and output during 1927 was on course for greater tonnage. However this mine was not meant to be an easy investment. At Christmas 1926, a creek flooded the mine, adding to operating costs. Then the main shaft met a fault and the coal seam was lost, requiring expensive tunneling. This was followed by a union dispute on Hobart's waterfront. When the mine company refused to pay the unloading rates demanded, the mine shut down. Reopening in 1928, it closed two years later when the company became bankrupt.

The seventh company to try its luck on the coalfield was formed in 1931. It abandoned the previous ship loading plant and transferred operations to a small wharf constructed at Waterhole Cove. A new mine location also was chosen. Despite the annual production of some 10,000 tons, misfortune struck when the company's tunnel also met a fault. This mine finally stopped production in 1939, the year in which the Leprena sawmill closed. Catamaran resumed its life as a ghost town, a future archaeological prospect and a symbol of undercapitalised ambition.

James Craig

The Catamaran Coal Mining Company purchased the *James Craig* in late 1925 and towed the hulk to Recherche Bay to serve as a bunker for the coal brought to the wharf. Within two years the vessel was found to be unsuitable for this function, so she was towed up to Coal Pit Bay and anchored near the French anchorage of 1792.

James Craig **(then the *Clan Macleod*), New York harbour 1890. Sydney Heritage Fleet**

The *James Craig*, then named the *Clan Macleod*, New York, 1890. Sydney Heritage Fleet

James Craig was built at Sutherland in 1873 as the *Clan Macleod*. Launched a year later, this square-rigger iron barque is a heritage item today, a rare survivor of the iron ships of the Clipper era. The nine decades that separated her construction from that of the *Recherche* reflect the immense technological progress within that period, even though the design harnessed wind power.[7]

The ship was constructed of wrought iron plates riveted on to iron frames and stringers. While her mizzenmast was pine, the two mainmasts and bowsprit were of iron; the tallest reached 35 metres. The interior of the iron plates was covered with cement as protection. Almost 55 metres long, the vessel's beam was nine metres and its hold was 5.5 metres deep. Access to the hold was gained through three hatches.

During the first quarter century, *Clan Macleod* sailed the world's trade routes carrying coal or general cargo. Her first voyage to Australia in 1879 carried British general cargo to Brisbane. As the years passed competition increased from coal driven steamships, which were faster and more reliable timewise.

An Auckland merchant and ship owner, J. J. Craig, bought the vessel in 1899, but he only renamed it after his son, James Craig, in 1905. Her first voyage was to take Australian Newcastle coal to Auckland. She made 34 trans-Tasman voyages until 1911, when she was purchased by the British New Guinea Development Company, and converted into a storage hulk in Port Moresby harbour.

ature*James Craig* submerged, 1960s, Recherche Bay. Sydney Heritage Fleet

The *James Craig* hulk resting in Recherche Bay in the 1960s, before its rescue during the early 1970s. Sydney Heritage Fleet

James Craig regained some standing because of World War 1 shipping shortage, when she was refitted and rerigged. A normal trading life seemed likely when she was purchased in 1918 by Henry Jones and Company, of IXL food. Unfortunately, she suffered damage en route to Sydney and was towed to port. A bad voyage to New Zealand followed. Then she was towed to Recherche Bay to await cargo, but none came. So she lay there at anchor. Eventually sold to the Catamaran Coal Mining Company and stripped down to her hull, her life as a coal bunker proved short. The derelict vessel was towed up the harbour and abandoned. Her second-last misfortune was to break her cable and drift. Then came disaster. As she was a hazard to other ships an enterprising fisherman blew a hole in her stern. She settled on the sandy and muddy bottom which d'Entrecasteaux had once judged excellent for holding the anchor. The stern was in five metres of water, while the prow stood high above the water. Sheltered in the harbour and its hull preserved below the seabed, *James Craig* survived there for nearly 40 years.

The hulk suffered senseless indignities during those forgotten decades. Vandals blew holes with gelignite in over a dozen places and an arsonist destroyed the decking; the above water iron plates rusted into a maze of holes. Recherche Bay slumbered as a vacation fishing harbour and on a favoured walking track south from Cockle Creek. This was the same path worn by generations of Aboriginal Tasmanians and followed by Labillardière's party to the south coast.

A Sydney group of historic ship lovers knew of the *James Craig* and feared that she might be refloated and taken to the San Francisco Maritime Museum. This was a time when modern technology offered a challenge to heritage ship lovers and maritime archaeologists to investigate or refloat sunken wrecks. The world looked on in wonderment when, in 1970, television screens showed Isambard Brunel's leviathan, the wrought iron *Great Britain* brilliantly rescued and refloated in the Falkland Islands. Viewers saw it being towed up the river from Avonmouth to the Bristol dry dock in which she had been built 130 years earlier.

Australian waters around 1970 also provided exciting discoveries. First came the retrieval of James Cook's *Endeavour* cannons from the Barrier Reef. Off Western Australia, Dutch shipwrecks were located and excavated beneath the sea. The first ship was *Vergulde Draeck* in 1972 and the *Batavia* followed.

It was March 1972 when *James Craig's* challenge was accepted by a group of Sydney and Tasmanian volunteers who patched holes and made a sandbag coffer dam near the stern to negate the three metre wide hole blasted in the stern. The long task of pumping out the water from this leaky hull commenced.

A salvage team arrived in October 1972 and the ship gradually started to rise from the natural moorings in which she was embedded. By May 1973 the hull was in a sufficiently repaired condition to stand the strains of towing. The tug *Sirius Cove* nudged the ship out of her Recherche Bay homeport and towed it to Hobart.

Funding restoration and a place where she might be permanently berthed proved to be difficult and changing problems over many years. Eventually *James Craig* was towed to Sydney. The decision by the Sydney Heritage Fleet organisation to totally restore the vessel so that it was capable of sailing with passengers posed problems. How authentic? Compromises were necessary without changing the basic appearance, using some excellent historic photographs of the vessel in her heyday. Mild steel substituted for wrought iron for those plates that required replacement; to meet contemporary regulations engines, shafts and propellers were fitted. This seems a practical solution to endow a rusty hull with decking, masts and people, but 'authenticity' is questionable.

The 1873 owner-financier of *Clan Macleod* would be intrigued, however, to learn that the restoration of his craft cost 12.5 million dollars. It is a reflection on the preconceptions or bias of Australian society that material objects — houses, ships, city landmarks — readily attract supporters, defenders and fund raisers. The preservation of the heritage values of the cultural landscape at Recherche Bay are more intangible — symbolic friendly racial contact, descriptions of lost Aboriginal lifeways, a landscape symbolic of the first European experience and their philosophical preconceptions, archaeological sites hidden within forests — but are they any less important or worth funding because they are more elusive and thought-provoking?

ENDNOTES

[1] In an unpublished consultant report Parry Kostoglou produced an excellent study of historic timber getting between Cockle Creek and Lune River (1993), which included clear maps of the tramways. Whitham (1983) did the same for the Catamaran Colliery. Bruce Poulson's short history of Recherche Bay contains excellent data on social life of residents around the bay.

[2] Dunbar in Gee and Fenton (eds), *The South West Book*, 1978: 34.

[3] Kostoglou, 'Historic timber-getting', 1993. This unpublished archaeological report contains a wealth of historical and contemporary images, which show the extent of surviving remains.

[4] On coal mining, see Whitham, *Papers and Proceedings Tasmanian Historical Research Association* 30 (1983).

[5] Twelvetrees, *Report on the coalfield in the neighbourhood of Recherche Bay*, 1902: 7.

[6] This, and the following information are based upon Twelvetrees, 1902 and Whitham, 1983.

[7] The following account of the *James Craig* draws upon Toghill, 1978 *The James Craig*, and Richards, 2000 *Signals* 52.

Chapter 14: The Concept of Heritage

Australians came late to the realisation that their natural environment and the historical imprint of past generations upon the landscape were valued possessions to treasure. Such features comprised not only material traces, such as forests, geological monuments, buildings, ruins or archaeological sites, but also intangibles associated with past persons or events, symbolic of ideas, memory or spirituality.

Such intangible or non-material factors present alternative considerations, additional to potential economic development or that overworked catch-cry of 'jobs'. When carefully assessed, these valued places may provide different opportunities for employment or development, such as tourism. Even when they cannot, once-off economic investment or temporary employment should not be the sole criterion in a balanced approach to Australia's long-term cultural or ecological future.

A national sense of purpose in firming concepts of heritage became evident about 40 years ago. There was a coincidence in timing around 1965 of the formation of the Australian Conservation Foundation, the Australian Council of National Trusts, the Australian Institute of Aboriginal Studies (now AIATSIS) and, in South Australia, the first State to enact legislation (tentatively) aimed to regulate the preservation of Aboriginal and early historic places.

The landmark in Federal government cultural and environmental maturity was the Whitlam Labor government appointment of the Hope Inquiry into the National Estate, 1973-74. In an investigation unprecedented internationally, this report evaluated equally the wellbeing and future of the trio: the natural environment, Aboriginal places, and historical structures and landscapes. In its succinct letter to the Prime Minister following this stocktaking came a challenge: 'here is our report on the nature and state of the National Estate and the means of conserving and presenting it'.[1]

At the national level, the response resulted in the creation of the Australian Heritage Commission. Before its enactment, this statutory authority was modified by the incoming Fraser administration, but it was passed with bipartisan support. The Commission operated from 1976 and I had the honour to be appointed as an inaugural Heritage Commissioner. In those times UNESCO (United Nations Educational, Scientific and Cultural Organisation) and its two advisory bodies, IUCN (International Union for the Conservation of Nature and Natural Resources) on environmental issues, and ICOMOS (International Council on Monuments and Sites) on cultural matters, were institutions respected by the Australian government. Heritage Commissioners approved of the 1960 UNESCO recommendation concerning the Protection of Cultural Property Endangered by Public or Private Works. Its advice was cited in the Hope Report:

> Cultural property is the product and witness of the different traditions and of the spiritual achievements of the past and is thus an essential element in the personality of the peoples of the world. It is the duty of governments to ensure the protection and preservation of the cultural heritage of mankind, as much as to promote social and economic development.[2]

UNESCO's sage advice on cost and benefit analysis is relevant to the issue of heritage components at Recherche Bay. The National Estate Inquiry recognised that it was difficult to quantify major conservation issues in a manner acceptable to a corporate boardroom. They stated firmly: 'Subjective factors must enter into any decision, first on whether a building, group of buildings or natural area is worthy of preservation in the national interest; second on the real long-term costs of preserving it, or of deciding not to do so.'[3] The crucial question posed was: 'Can we afford, in the long-term, to lose it?' To answer such a question requires systematic and objective field survey and documentary research, expert discussion of the pros and cons independent of political interference.

An election was fought in 1983 with this question in mind, the consequences of damming the Franklin River. A comparable question has dominated the last three years, although the media chose to ignore the issues on the mainland. Even when Recherche Bay featured prominently on Tasmanian ABC television and radio, mainlanders largely were kept in ignorance of this nationally significant matter. Similarly, in Hobart, while *The Mercury* and the *Sunday Tasmanian* frequently reported relevant developments, mainland newspapers rarely commented. This was not a parochial matter, but the media judged it to be so. The media should remember that Australia is a Federation and not a confusion of isolationist or uncaring States.

Following the creation of the Australian Heritage Commission, it was anticipated that the States would enact complementary legislation embracing the Natural, Cultural and Aboriginal environments. This was slow to eventuate, except in New South Wales, Victoria and South Australia. Such legislation also experienced different emphases, including adequate staffing, comprehensive coverage and the political will to implement it. Tasmania was said to be considering legislation in 1981, but it was not carried until 1995.[4] The Tasmanian Heritage Council of 15 members resolved 'to advise the Minister on matters relating to Tasmania's historic cultural heritage and measures necessary to conserve that heritage'.

In 1979, Australia ICOMOS, a recently established branch of the UNESCO cultural heritage advisory body, acting in cooperation with the Australian Heritage Commission, produced the Burra Charter, a guide to cultural heritage ethics and conservation practice.⁵ This charter has undergone evolutionary changes as practitioners better appreciate the great variety of heritage issues, both ethical and practical.

Within recent years, the concept of an entity termed 'cultural landscape' has emerged in international circles on the philosophy of heritage conservation. Rather than the normal listing of individual structures or elements, they often are better appreciated within a broad context of human activities and their consequences. The concept applies to landscapes that have been modified through human actions over time. Its focus is on the relationship between people and place.

Recherche Bay is such a cultural landscape. Although it was known as the French landing place, its role in providing a palimpsest of Tasmanian history was neglected until recently. It was the reported discovery of Delahaye's 1792 garden, in January 2003, that highlighted the potential significance of the area. Whether it really was the garden became less important when historical sources were consulted on the totality of the French visits. In my case, it was the realisation that this 'moment of contact' between Europeans and Tasmanians took place across a confined area. The records of those encounters are vital for the human story in Tasmania. The French expedition undertook scientific studies, while subsequent European activities across almost two centuries left imprints upon the landscape, although often concealed beneath vegetation. It is important to stress that my reaction, and that of most people, was not an attack upon the forest industry or the rights of landowners. It simply was that this small area was too significant to destroy.

In 1992 the World Heritage Committee of UNESCO adopted modifications to the World Heritage cultural criteria drawn up in Paris in 1977 (at which I was an Australian delegate). It adopted a broad definition of cultural landscapes, consisting of three dynamic categories. The first consists of a landscape deliberately designed and created, such as those eighteenth century British landscapes created for nobility by Capability Brown. A second category is an organically evolved landscape, where continuing but unintentional human interaction creates a new landscape, such as Kangaroo Valley, New South Wales. The third class is an associative cultural landscape, such as New Norcia, Western Australia.

Recherche Bay fits the last definition. It has been modified through the various industrial and occupational activities across two centuries and archaeological evidence survives for each phase. Also associated are traces of Aboriginal occupation and links with significant events and people. Such associations include the d'Entrecasteaux episodes and interaction with the Aboriginal Tasmanian population. Then there is the connection with European science through Labillardière, Rossel and Beautemps-Beaupré. Even the visit by Lady

Jane Franklin and John Gould are linkages symbolic of notable people. Recherche Bay could truly be termed Tasmania's Botany Bay.

Such reasoning implies that concepts require updating, to bring cultural landscapes within an Australian definition in order to include places of intangible but symbolic significance, even though physical traces may seem unimpressive. This is surely the case already with Captain Cook's landing place at Botany Bay, or the Burke and Wills 'dig tree' on Cooper's Creek. So why not the d'Entrecasteaux landing place?

The problem is that much Australian legislation has failed to keep pace with such changing international concepts as the category of a cultural landscape. Consequently, opponents of listing such a place are offered an easy legal technicality. As there is no reference in the relevant State Act to such a definition, this conveniently rules it out of consideration. Consequently, in 2004, Ken Bacon, Tasmanian Minister for Tourism, Parks and Heritage, stated that 'the advice from his Department is that the existing *Historic Cultural Heritage Act* 1995 does not enable him to consider the issue of cultural landscapes'. As part of a current legislative review, however, he wisely requested that this matter be considered.[6] The reality is, however, that the minister and his government lacked the political will to accede, and sought excuses.

Despite the minister's expedient decision, the *Historic Cultural Heritage Act* includes a definition of a 'place', to include a 'precinct or parcel of land' (1, 3). Given ministerial will there were ways around this technicality. Criteria for entry in the Tasmanian Register include those that admirably fit the Aboriginal significance of this place (a cultural landscape without applying that term)

- 16 (c) 'it has potential to yield information that will contribute to an understanding of Tasmania's history'.
- 16 (f) 'it has strong or special meaning for any group or community because of social, cultural or spiritual association'.
- 16 (g) 'it has special association with the life or work of a person, a group or an organization that was important in Tasmania's history'.

This surely describes the significant roles played by d'Entrecasteaux, Labillardière, Rossel and Beautemps-Beaupré.

It is obvious that the Tasmanian government used 'cultural landscape' as a device to obscure adopting one or more of the above options. Behind this facade loomed the *Forest Practices Act* 1985, the *Tasmanian Regional Forest Agreement* 1997 and the *Forest Practices Code* set up under the Act. The Forest Agreement separated the timber industry from all other industries and heritage considerations. The *Forest Practices Code* provides that industry with independence, so concerning heritage matters (including cultural heritage), it became a self-investigating and self-approval granting authority.

The Chair of the Tasmanian Heritage Council proved more outspoken than the minister, when he stated in 2003:

> Listing [of part of Recherche Bay] would protect everything except forest practices. We can't control forest practices because they're specifically excluded. So listing is virtually pointless in this situation.[7]

Surely the Commonwealth government ignored prudent administration of cultural heritage, if not natural heritage justice also, by agreeing to this monopolistic agreement outside the mainstream approval process. Presumably another consideration within Tasmania's government was the reluctance to set a precedent by paying compensation to private landowners when conservation issues require cessation of logging.

Much of the land surrounding Recherche Bay was surveyed and subdivided for private sale from the 1830s, when ambitious plans resulted in the layout of the abortive township of Ramsgate on the south-western shore. The 1863 survey of the north-eastern peninsula suggests that much of the land had been sold, while Bennetts Point bore its present name.

The area that was harvested for the Leprena mill has been largely included in the 4,280 hectare Southport Lagoon Wildlife Sanctuary, proclaimed in 1976 and subsequently expanded. It includes Southport and Blackswan Lagoons and a coastline of some 16 kilometres. It is a poorly drained area supporting an unusual complex of heath, sedgeland and forest communities. As this and the private land on the peninsula provided the floral collection ground for Labillardière, it is the type locality for many Australian plants and therefore an important biological reference area. The Sanctuary also is an important waterfowl habitat and breeding area. It was the numerous black swans reported, drawn (and eaten) by the d'Entrecasteaux personnel which are believed to have inspired Delahaye to introduce black swans into Empress Josephine's Malmaison gardens in Paris. Innumerable black swans can still be seen today on the surface of Blackswan Lagoon, so it was truly well named.

Southport Lagoon Wildlife Sanctuary is the refuge for *Euphrasia gibbsiae* subsp. *psilanthera*, swamp eyebright, a short-lived perennial herb listed through the *Environment Protection and Biodiversity Conservation Act* 1999 as a Critically Endangered plant. Its *only* known occurrence is a 50 by 50 metre area north-east of Blackswan Lagoon. It was listed in the *Tasmanian Regional Forest Agreement* 1997 (attachment 2, part B), consequently by ignoring its presence to construct an access road surely violated that Agreement. Another plant species that grows only in Tasmania, *Thelymitra jonesii* (sky-blue sun orchid), is approaching critical endangered status.

The Sanctuary was included on the Register of the National Estate in 1978. The 146-hectare area then owned by David and Robert Vernon is bordered on two sides by this Sanctuary and access to their land could be gained only through the Sanctuary. Conservation prudence would have suggested the acquisition of their land at an early stage, either from relevant State or Commonwealth budgets, and its incorporation within the Sanctuary.

The owners had acted correctly under the terms of the *Forest Practices Act* when they declared their property a Private Timber Reserve. It was then gazetted in 1996 as a Private Timber Reserve. They also stated that known heritage places would be protected.[8] Although the Recherche Bay Protection Group was formed before the discovery of the 'garden' in 2003, because it was aware of the historical value of the area, more widespread awareness followed news of Delahaye's garden. Perhaps that site should have been recorded long ago, but concern for historical archaeological field evidence only developed since the 1970s. Australia is a vast continent and workers in the archaeological research vineyard were few. (I was the first person at an Australian university to teach the pre-1788 history and archaeology of Australia and the Pacific, at the University of Melbourne in 1957. A decade later Historical Archaeology was first offered at the University of Sydney).

During my public and written interventions in controversies across the past three years, I stressed that the owners should be adequately recompensed should their property be acquired for the nation. I strictly observed their ban on my entering their property, following my first visit in February 2003. The ABC program, *Catalyst*, was filmed entirely on the beach later that year. Although they have claimed in the media that I encouraged people to invade their property on the occasion of the rally in April 2005, there are witnesses who can testify to the fact that I urged the very opposite, to the annoyance of some enthusiasts.

The obvious requirement, given the claims that the French garden had been located, was for archaeological research to test that claim. In February 2003, when the Heritage Council first discussed the matter it was stated that the Council lacked any funds for such a purpose. Neither the State nor the Commonwealth authorities bothered to consider funding field research. Three years later no fieldwork had been attempted, although subsequent to the completion of this text, archaeological fieldwork has been carried out, but so far is unreported.

Acting in ignorance of the existence of any archaeological evidence, except for the 'garden' and the observatory area, it was easy to claim that no other sites existed. Consequently, Minister Ken Bacon conceived a compromise solution. On 14 October 2004 he announced the establishment of a 100 metre protection zone around the coastline of the north-eastern peninsula and an additional 100 metre zone around the garden and the observatory sites.[9] The listing applied for five years, allowing time for 'heritage surveys', but 15 months later no survey had been attempted. In the same news release, the minister granted permission for the landowners to construct an access road through the Southport Lagoon

Wildlife Conservation Area. All this despite his admission that 'further work is required to appreciate the area's full significance'.[10]

The logging access track was constructed across the Conservation Area. When I visited there in April 2005, it appeared to violate the soil erosion precautionary procedures required by ignoring contours in the land and leaving gaping stretches in the banks beside the road. Such banks were intended to obstruct four-wheel drive access to the Area, but from the many tyre tracks they facilitated it. This made a mockery of the term 'Conservation Area'.

The logging track through Southport Lagoon Conservation Area, 2005. Senator Bob Brown

The unfinished logging road bulldozed across the Southport Lagoon Conservation Area, 2002. Photograph by Senator Bob Brown

The Parks and Wildlife Service Tasmania, a branch of the minister's own department, made available a draft management plan for public comment in July 2005. The cover image was the endangered swamp eyebright. In a discussion of management issues the report notes that: the plant grows 'next to a vehicle track … the resulting track braiding is threatening the extinction of the species';[11] also there is increasing risk from *Phytophthora* invasion, facilitated by vehicles. It is clear that the minister's decision was contrary to any concept of best practice for park management. The draft management plan goes on to stress that: 'Physical damage caused by the use of recreational vehicle [sic] is by far the single biggest management issue in the conservation area.' In places tracks are up to 500 metres wide where drivers have avoided bogs or deliberately created 'mud play' areas.[12] This new track has opened up new areas to destruction.

Upon a visit to the area in March 2006, I noted the damage caused by four-wheel drive vehicles, together with erosion, along this track. Elsewhere, on the south-eastern part of the peninsula, it is heart-wrenching to walk the area between Quiet Cove and Blackswan Lagoon, which four-wheel drivers treat as their own. Dozens of empty beer cans strew the area where the French and Tasmanians fraternised in 1793. North-west of the bay, part of the Leprena track was impassable due to the mud games played by these irresponsible drivers.

Permission having been granted to harvest the timber, on 6 April 2005, the Secretary of the Department of Tourism, Parks, Heritage and the Arts, Mr S. Gadd, informed the Commonwealth Department of Environment and Heritage of the safeguards proposed. Citing the *Forest Practices Code*, he stated that the Forest Practices Board Senior Archaeologist would 'undertake periodic inspections during operations'. Discovery of 'any new historic features' would result in cessation of operations near that feature and the archaeologist would be summoned.[13] That heavy machinery moving through the landscape would leave 'features' intact is impossible, or that workmen would be able to recognise one is equally implausible. I was quoted in *The Mercury* as dismissing the proposal as 'stupidity', and I emphatically repeat that verdict here.[14] It reveals the *Forest Practices Code* for what it is, a high sounding but hollow policy designed to access timber with token attention to cultural heritage.

It is time to discuss the Howard Coalition government attitude to heritage issues. In its stance over international heritage concerns its policy is at variance with that of previous administrations. It is best described today as an unfortunate isolationist nationalism. This was highlighted in 1998-99, when an expert UNESCO committee reported upon the potential adverse impact of uranium mining at Jabiluka upon the World Heritage Kakadu National Park. The committee firmly recommended that it should be listed on the 'World Heritage in Danger' register.

The government's reaction was one of no-holds-barred. It denigrated the expertise of the prestigious committee, having ensured that during its visit to Kakadu the committee's contact with critics was minimal. As a person giving evidence to that committee I can vouch for the contrivances employed by the host department to achieve that end. Nations on the World Heritage executive committee were extensively lobbied while taxpayers funded a three-week visit to Paris by the minister and several senior staffers. They secured a reversal of the recommendation. Meantime, Australia ICOMOS, expert advisor to Paris ICOMOS on cultural matters, was represented in Paris by a conscientious self-funded member.[15]

It possibly was government petulance over this affair that contributed to its decision to abolish the independent statutory authority, the Australian Heritage Commission. In its original scheme the government proposed also to scrap the Register of the National Estate. This list of over 13,000 places worth keeping was a prudential stocktake. It is not legally binding, but it does pose a moral reminder to developers and the public. It was intended to abandon the Register as a Commonwealth entity and return relevant listed places to individual State control.

For some States this was possibly an acceptable outcome, but notoriously inappropriate for others. A reading of the *Tasmanian Forest Agreement* 1997, attachment 1 (7-11), for example, gives cause for concern. Note the cosy comment by Tasmanian Resources Minister, Bryan Green, on Recherche Bay, concerning cultural heritage and biodiversity: 'the forest practices and management system has ensured all those protections are afforded'.[16] In the final outcome, in the face of much criticism, the Commonwealth wisely agreed to retain the Register of the National Estate. Consequently, under the *Environment Protection and Biodiversity Conservation Act* 1999, the minister must have regard to information in the Register before making any decision to which the information is relevant. The access road to the peninsula ignored the Register list.

The Australian Heritage Council Act 2003 came into force early in 2004. Like the Tasmanian Heritage Council, it has been gelded, because it is only advisory and the minister is not obliged to take its advice. At the same time, the *Environment and Heritage Legislation Amendment Act* incorporated relevant matters in the *Environment Protection and Biodiversity Conservation Act*. Amendments to that Act late in 2006 regrettably abolished the Register of the National Estate conflicting with earlier promises to retain it. While it is a relief that the inspirational and historical landscape at Recherche Bay is now a registered National Heritage place, the future of many places on the Register of the National Estate is less promising.

ENDNOTES

[1] *Report of the National Estate* (The Hope Inquiry), Canberra: AGPS, 1974: 1, 25, 29.
[2] Ibid.
[3] Ibid.
[4] *Australia's National Estate*. Special Australian Heritage Publication series Number 1, Canberra: AGPS, 1985: 136; *Historical Cultural Heritage Act* 1995.
[5] Marquis-Kyle and Walker, *The Illustrated Burra Charter*, 2004, is the latest version.
[6] *The Mercury*, 14 October 2004.
[7] *The Mercury*, 4 November 2003; press statement 19 November 2003.
[8] Media release by D. and R. Vernon, 20 February 2003.
[9] Media release by Ken Bacon, 14 October 2004.
[10] Ibid.
[11] Southport Lagoon conservation Area, Draft Management Plan, 2005: 10, 47.
[12] Ibid.

13 *The Mercury*, 13 April 2005.
14 *The Mercury*, 17 April 2005.
15 Mulvaney, *Dissent* 7 (2001/2002): 47-50.
16 ABC Online, 17 April 2005.

Chapter 15: National Heritage Nomination

Under the new Heritage legislation nominations are invited for places to gain National Heritage status. Following evaluation by the Heritage Council, its advice is given to the minister. During the first week that the Act came into force, February 2004, I nominated the north-eastern peninsula of Recherche Bay. This was the main area of contact between the French and the Tasmanians, the collecting ground for flora, the location of the vegetable garden and scene of the geomagnetic observations. It also was the area likely to be destroyed. While the entire harbour has heritage values and merits listing, greater research was necessary at that time before a convincing nomination could be made.

I now realise that my nomination should have been elaborated to make a better case. However, as I had prepared a paper in June 2003 for the National Cultural Heritage Forum, which was discussed at length in the presence of the then Minister, Dr David Kemp, and contributed to a staff seminar at the Department of Environment and Heritage, I assumed that the data and significance were well understood in the Department. Further, I published two articles canvassing the subject in the *Canberra Times* [1] The *Environment and Heritage Legislative Amendment Act* 2003 provides that the minister may 'ask the person who nominated the place to provide additional information' [324E(4)]. I was never asked.

Subsequently the minister received at least two requests for the immediate emergency listing of the place in view of the announced plan to harvest timber across the peninsula. The minister must have received considerable expert opinion during the lengthy 20 months between my nomination and the announcement in October 2005 that the place was granted National Heritage List status. To my knowledge this included letters from the Presidents of the prestigious Australian Academy of Science and the Australian Academy of the Humanities. Several other Academy Fellows and scientists presented pleas, as did the Chair of the Australian Council of National Trusts and the Director of Research, Australian Institute of Aboriginal and Torres Strait Islander Studies. The Ambassador of France, His Excellency Patrick Hénault, actively pursued matters relating to the presence of the d'Entrecasteaux expedition, even personally visiting Recherche Bay and facilitating a visit to the site by Hélène Richard from the Bibliothèque Nationale de France and author of a valuable book on the d'Entrecasteaux expedition. Accompanying her was Jean-Christophe Galipaud, an archaeologist working on the La Pérouse wreck site on Vanikoro Island. He returned in 2006 and conducted excavations, but these are so far unreported.

'The axe had never sounded'

The Chair of the Australian Council of National Trusts, Simon Molesworth, was active in attempts to convince the Commonwealth government to buy the land. His Council ranked Recherche Bay amongst the top ten historic sites in the nation. 'Let's not tinker around the edges,' he stressed, 'This site is as significant as the *Mayflower* and the landing [site] of the First Fleet.'[2] Dr Hugh Tyndale-Biscoe, a senior CSIRO biologist, published an article in the *Australian Academy of Science Newsletter* under the title 'a site of great significance'.[3]

Unfortunately politicians of all the main parties tend to scorn interventions by Senator Bob Brown and sneer at Greens Party expectations. Despite the vitriol poured by the Tasmanian timber interests and so readily marketed by the media, Brown and the Tasmanian Greens merit praise for their stand. These were not politically mischievous schemes to harm the timber industry and its employees. Tasmania is a political jungle where the critics do not see the valuable historical wood for the commercially exploitive trees. It is testimony to their sincerity that Bob Brown self-funded a fine photographic essay and booklet on Recherche Bay,[4] while future Senator Christine Milne engaged in research in Paris on gardener Delahaye. Few of their parliamentary critics genuinely invest as much in heritage and environmental concerns. It is fitting that Dick Smith, whose environmental interests are well known, should accept the validity of Bob Brown's approach and agree to assist to funding the purchase of the land.

At the local level in Tasmania, the debate over the Bay's future engendered deep community concern — this was not the plot of a few Greens. Senator Eric Abetz, Federal Forestry and Conservation Minister, should feel ashamed of his outburst upon learning that this small timbered area would be preserved: 'Recherche Bay has no biodiversity worth conserving,'[5] is a statement based upon ignorance and bias. The Register of the National Estate contains sufficient evidence to refute Abetz, particularly if the Southport Conservation Area is included, through which the timber access road winds for about three kilometres. Consider, also, the rally beside this track which scars the environment. In April 2005, almost 1,000 people assembled there on a Sunday morning to vote literally with their feet and to express their outrage.

Such popular support had been spearheaded by citizens living in the Huon region (some of whom feared threats to vandalise their homes). Calling itself the Recherche Bay Protection Group, it sponsored a meeting in Southport as early as November 2002.[6] This meeting of 70 people assembled some weeks before the discovery of the supposed garden received interstate media attention.

Mulvaney addressing the April 2005 rally. Tom Baxter

John Mulvaney addressing the protest rally near Recherche Bay, April 2005. Photograph by Tom Baxter

One of the discoverers of this site, Bruce Poulson, in 2004 published a well-researched and illustrated history of Recherche Bay. He demonstrated that this was a genuinely significant place in Aboriginal and European Australian history. That commercial logging interests persisted in their plans to harvest timber suggests that issues of cultural heritage are not a priority.

A group of local enthusiasts produced a play centred around Louise Gerardin. Another group of local female musicians showed imagination and verve by forming The Recherche Baybes group. They dressed in French period costumes and sang witty refrains such as the following words dedicated to gardener Delahaye. They attracted widespread interest.[7] The point is that there was deep grass roots concern within the Tasmanian community which government ignored at its peril.

Le Jardin

by the Recherche Baybes

Chorus

Nine by seven
It's nine by seven
Grey mossy rocks
Laid out in straight lines
And divided in four by a gardener's hand

'The axe had never sounded'

A lovely French garden in our Southern land.
In seventeen-hundred and ninety-two
The *Recherche* and *Espérance* with scientists and crew
Found a beautiful harbour in Van Diemen's Land
The best things in life are so rarely planned.

There was water and wood and shellfish and game
And wondrous plants to study and name
The astronomers charted the stars by night
The mapmakers charted each island and bight.

The gardener on board was young Felix LaHaye
At times his thoughts fled to his home far away
I will build a garden that's pretty and neat
Overlooking the bay where the soil is sweet.

Chorus

He paced out the plot and he called for some aid
They dug up the ground and the stones they did lay
He planted some cabbages, sorrel and peas
So Indigenous people could harvest with ease.

Several weeks later they all sailed away
Returning again eight months to the day
Young Felix returned to his garden fair
And was saddened to find there was so little there.

Some of the plants were stunted and pale
The weeds and the weather'd insured that they'd fail
But he gathered potatoes and lettuce and cress
While wallabies made a meal of the rest.

Chorus

The quiet returned to the plot on the Bay
The Indigenous people were driven away
The fires they razed the last of the plants
Long after young Felix returned home to France.

Many years on as history passed by
The rocks in the garden were lost to the sky
Protected and safe as the trees grew around
Just waiting for the moment that they would be found.

The sound of the bulldozers were coming this way
To threaten the garden o'erlooking the Bay
Old Felix LaHaye he stirred in his grave

You must do what you can, my garden to save.

Some kind, caring people came looking around
Then one of them saw the stones on the ground
They were all lying there from the first to the last
Young Felix's garden, a gift from the past.

Chorus x 2

The Environment and Heritage Legislation Amendment Act (NOI) 2003 stated that 'a place may be included in the National Heritage List only if the minister is satisfied that the place has one or more National Heritage values' (324C, 2). However, only one National Heritage value is required to meet the criteria (324D, 1). The Australian Heritage Council is obliged to assess and convey its advice to the minister within twelve months of his request (324G, 2).

Under this Act, provision exists for emergency declaration should a place be in imminent risk of destruction. Through 2004, when timber harvesting appeared probable, the place was at risk. Concerned groups applied to have the area declared under the emergency legislation. It is stressed that it was the *risk* to the place, and not its heritage values, which required a ministerial decision.

Minister Ian Campbell's decision not to include the north-east peninsula under the Act's emergency provision was announced on 28 January 2005. It mentions that the Heritage Council had advised him on 22 October 2004 (par. 25) that the 'place might have one or more National Heritage values'.[8] In fact, a reading of his report indicates that seven values met possibly five of the criteria in the Council's opinion. Even so, one year elapsed before it was listed as a National Heritage place in October 2005, making the time elapsed since nomination 20 months. For supporters like myself it proved a fraught time, but another four months elapsed before the place was secured from timber harvesting and so preserved for future Australians.

In light of the evidence surveyed in the early chapters of this book it is appropriate to examine the reasons given by the minister in January 2005 for rejecting the listing under emergency provisions. Under section 324D of the Act the criteria for listing are as follows:

The National Heritage criteria for a place are any or all of the following:

a. the place has outstanding heritage value to the nation because of the place's importance in the course, or pattern, of Australia's natural or cultural history;
b. the place has outstanding heritage value to the nation because of the place's possession of uncommon, rare or endangered species of Australia's natural or cultural history;

c. the place has outstanding heritage value to the nation because of the place's potential to yield information that will contribute to an understanding of Australia's natural or cultural history;
d. the place has outstanding heritage value to the nation because of the place's importance in demonstrating the principal characteristics of:
   i. a class of Australia's natural or cultural places; or
   ii. a class of Australia's natural or cultural environments;
e. the place has outstanding heritage value to the nation because of the place's importance in exhibiting particular aesthetic characteristics valued by a community or group;
f. the place has outstanding heritage value to the nation because of the place's importance in demonstrating a high degree or creative or technical achievement at a particular period;
g. the place has outstanding heritage value to the nation because of the place's strong or special association with a particular community or cultural group for social, cultural or spiritual reasons;
h. the place has outstanding heritage value to the nation because of the place's special association with the life or works of a person, or group of persons, of importance in Australia's natural or cultural history;
i. the place has outstanding heritage value to the nation because of the place's importance as part of indigenous tradition.

The minister's decision was conveyed in a detailed 23-page document.[9] Firstly, consider the criteria accepted by the minister:

- Because of the importance, nature and records of the French contact with Tasmanians, the minister agreed that this probably met criterion (a).
- So also, Labillardière's botanical collection could meet (a).
- If investigations confirmed the garden site it might meet criterion (b).
- Rossel's geomagnetic measurements were sufficiently important to meet criterion (f).
- The area's association with the Aboriginal community for social, cultural and spiritual reasons may meet criterion (g).
- Association with Labillardière's work probably meets criterion (h).
- The same applies to Rossel (h).

Consequently, in January 2005, the north-eastern peninsula was seen to probably possess National Heritage values under criteria (a), (b), (f), (g) and (h). Only one criterion under the Act is required for listing. However, the minister refused listing under the Emergency provision. A summary of his reasons would include the following: the major encounters with the Aborigines occurred outside the boundary of the private land; the 100 metre buffer zone protected the known features; the *Forest Practices Code* ensured adequate identification and protection should new evidence be uncovered during timber harvesting.

I turn now to discuss those features in the nomination which the minister rejected:

- The assessment ignored the evidence that both French and Aborigines criss-crossed over the peninsula, so that camping places or material objects may exist, and would be hopelessly disturbed, by modern timber harvesting techniques.
- Piron's art was rejected as significant because, it was asserted, Piron did not depict 'hard primitives', but classical figures. Readers should consult the plates in this book and note the detailed ethnography of Tasmanian society at this dramatic moment of first contact. Other meetings with British crews are mentioned as being friendly, but none were as 'friendly' as this episode. While allowance should be made for the possibility that the engraver accentuated the conventions of classical art. This was a one-off record of Tasmanian life as it was.
- The minister deferred consideration on whether the area constitutes a cultural landscape. It is a priority for the Australian Heritage Council to produce criteria for assessing cultural landscapes. They must include associations with intangible significant persons, concepts and symbols. Such criteria are explained in the 2004 *Illustrated Burra Charter* of Australia ICOMOS.
- The evidence for the floral diversity and integrity of the area is questioned. Undeniably this is an area of regrowth, but the harvesting was by less-damaging traditional pre-1940 methods. Despite the minister's doubts, this is the type site for type specimens which still survive in European museums, so the area is a potential biological reference which may become relevant in the future. Prudence would retain it.
- The question of a cultural landscape association with *Eucalyptus globulus* merits consideration. This species is grown widely around the world and is the tree by which eucalypts are best known. (What species did Mussolini and his predecessors plant to drain the Pontine marshes?)
- It was in the assessment of Beautemps-Beaupré's hydrographic survey that the minister's decision was surprising. He ruled that this survey did not confer outstanding heritage value to the nation under criterion (f). This survey demonstrated that Bruny and other islands were separated from Tasmania, while d'Entrecasteaux Channel opened a new and shorter route to eastern Australia and the future Hobart. New instruments and new surveying techniques were applied here first, before sailing to Santa Cruz. That the minister stated that this latter smaller island was used by Beautemps-Beaupré to illustrate a model application of his techniques is hardly relevant. An island offered a more convenient example than a long

and sinuous channel. It is the quality of the work and its consequences that matter. Remember, also, that Flinders thought this survey the best ever done in a new country. As Recherche Bay was the base for most of this survey, it offers another cultural association.

The point of all this discussion is that a reassessment in the light of the evidence provided in this book would confirm all those criteria accepted as probable by the minister, but add further to that list. It was placed on the National Heritage List on 7 October 2005, essentially following those elements that were discussed and accepted in the minister's rejection of the previous discussion. Surveying remained unrewarded. It met criteria (a), (c), (f), (g) and (h), criterion (c) replacing (b) of the emergency provision. Tasmania's Recherche Bay is a place to cherish for all Australians.

The Dénouement

Senator Bob Brown completed three years of selfless campaigning to save the peninsula from logging with a desperate action. During November 2005, he circulated an appeal for pledged funding to purchase the land from the Vernon brothers. 'Unlike most of Tasmania's contentious forests,' he wrote, 'this one is privately owned. So it has an unusual rescue option: to buy it! We are aiming to do this by public subscription. I am writing to seek your help.'[10]

While many wellwishers pledged contributions, in the circumstances this amounted to the equivalent of many widows' mites. The appeal became a practicality when Dick Smith contributed $100,000 with a promise to underwrite a further $1.9 million. If that sum was not subscribed and repaid within a year, he and his wife, Pip, generously promised to meet the budgetary deficit. Entrepreneur Dick Smith is a well-known global adventurer, a champion of things Australian and deeply interested in environmental issues. It possibly helped his decision that previously he spent some time at Recherche Bay in his boat. Like the French in 1792, he witnessed the awesome beauty of nature.

It is a sad reflection on Australian cultural mores that such altruism is so rare amongst wealthy Australians. In its relative isolation Smith's benefaction is magnified. 'I am not a rabid anti-logger,' Smith stated reasonably, 'and I understand that Tasmanians need to be employed. But this is an exceptional area of Tasmania ... that must be saved.'[11]

Following some weeks of negotiation between the owners, Bob Brown and the Tasmanian Land Conservancy, an amicable settlement was near. At this last minute the Tasmanian government decided to act positively. Only as recently as 12 December 2005, the Minister for Parks and Heritage, Judy Jackson, informed Bob Brown that the Tasmanian government would not provide any funds for land purchase. Obviously unaware of the archaeological issues at stake, she blandly relied upon the *Forest Practices Code* to ensure 'that any significant cultural heritage sites ... are conserved'.[12]

With the scent of a mid-March 2006 election in the air, the Premier, Paul Lennon, presumably smelt political advantage in making a total reversal of policy. This came after years of adverse policy towards this heritage place and determination to support the timber industry at any price. Evidently the fear of creating a precedent by saving this small, isolated property was forgotten. The irony of the Premier's verdict is best overlooked in the welcome relief of this positive outcome. 'This is a good result for Tasmania today and for future generations,' Premier Lennon observed, 'I'm pleased that commonsense has prevailed and we have been able to arrive at a sensible agreement.'[13] Indeed, those who fought to save the place for three years were pleased that commonsense finally prevailed.

Matters approached finality as this paragraph was being written. David and Robert Vernon merit praise for agreeing to this honourable solution, which presumably sees them both millionaires even though their three-year harvest of 30,000 tonnes of woodchips and 5,000 tonnes of sawlogs remain uncut. The Tasmanian government deserves credit for not only changing its policy, but for assisting financially, particularly with the costs of rehabilitation of the disastrous access logging road through the Southport Wildlife Conservation Area. Gunns Ltd is to be recompensed by $200,000.

While the north-eastern peninsula is now secure and could be considered for amalgamation into the Southport Wildlife Conservation Area, readers of this book will be aware of the extent of human activities around the Bay. In 1793 the French land operations were conducted around the shore in the Cockle Creek area. Somewhere in that vicinity the first European burial in Tasmania occurred, following the death of a French crew member. Around the shore lies evidence for at least 15 whaling sites; coal mining and timber milling were based near Catamaran and d'Entrecasteaux rivers; trackways trace networks through the forest; foundations of jetties disappear into the sea; through much of the twentieth century the homes and activities of communities who lived here have left archaeological traces.

During July 2005, Senator Ian Campbell, the Commonwealth Minister for Heritage and Environment, wisely visited Recherche Bay to experience the nature of the place for himself. He described his time there as 'absolutely fascinating'. As he toured the western and southern areas of the harbour, he correctly judged that my National Heritage nomination was deficient. 'While clearly the area has got a lot of protection from the Tasmanian Government,' he observed tactfully, 'I did indicate that I thought the heritage nomination was incomplete because it ignored or failed to incorporate some historic sites on the western side of the bay as well.'[14]

It is rewarding to learn that the minister requested the Australian Heritage Council to investigate the heritage claims of this area, part of the cultural landscape of the harbour. Unfortunately, prior to the heritage interest in Recherche Bay, the Tasmanian government granted a permit for an ecotourism development in the Cockle Creek area. It is an ambitious project with possibly 80 units, which could impact adversely upon the 1793 French occupation area and also impair the landscape vista, together with its necessary road system.

There is no doubt that the Tasmanian government now needs to re-evaluate this project and link it with a systematic management plan for the entire harbour precinct. There has been such publicity concerning the north-eastern peninsula, with more likely once archaeological investigations commence, that ecotourism is likely to burgeon. After all, it is only two hours drive from Hobart. It is important to ensure that such tourism is not piece-meal and management plans are developed for visitation to significant places.

So, the Recherche Bay saga has a happy ending, as it is now owned by the Tasmanian Land Conservancy. It is an object lesson to all governments and particularly timber and mining industries, that development or exploitative plans need to take significant cultural landscapes, or specific cultural assets, (even when intangible), into account before they announce projects. It proves less costly, less emotive and conserves heritage for future generations. While the sound of the axe was loud in these forests a century ago, the whirr of powered saws has been silenced in perpetuity. Should Labillardière return here even today, he could still sense the awe within this forested landscape and its mountainous backdrop. Now that its continued regeneration is assured, the tercentenary of the French arrival should produce a forested landscape on the peninsula approximating to that of 1792.

ENDNOTES

[1] *Canberra Times*, 17 Dec. 2003, 6 Sept. 2004; letter 31 Dec. 2003.
[2] *The Mercury*, 31 October 2004.
[3] Tyndale-Biscoe, *Australian Academy of Science Newsletter* 60 (2004): 3.
[4] Brown, *Tasmania's Recherche Bay*, 2005.
[5] ABC Online, 9 February 2006.
[6] Poulson, *Recherche Bay*, 2004: 75.
[7] Ibid.: 71.
[8] Statement of Reasons for Decision under section 324F of *The Environment Protection and Biodiversity Conservation Act* 1999. 28 January 2005.
[9] Ibid.
[10] Brown, circular
[11] *The Mercury*, 6 February 2006.
[12] J. Jackson, Minister for Parks and Heritage to B. Brown 12 December 2005.
[13] *The Mercury*, 9 February 2006.
[14] *The Mercury*, 6 July 2005.

References

Anderson, S., 2000, 'French anthropology in Australia, a prelude: the encounters between Aboriginal Tasmanians and the expedition of Bruny d'Entrecasteaux', *Aboriginal History* 24: 212–23.

Beautemps-Beaupré, C. F., 1807, *Atlas du voyage de Bruny-Dentrecasteaux*, Paris: Dépôt Général des Cartes et Plans.

Bonnemains, J., Forsyth, E. and Smith, B. (eds), 1988, *Baudin in Australian waters*, Melbourne: Oxford University Press.

Bowler, J. M., Johnston, H., et al., 2003, New ages for human occupation and climatic change at Lake Mungo, *Nature* 421: 837-840.

Brown, Bob, 2005, *Tasmania's Recherche Bay*, Hobart: Green Institute.

Carr, D. J. and S. G. M. (eds), 1981, *People and plants in Australia*, Sydney: Academic Press.

Clune, F. and Stephensen, P. R., 1962, *The pirates of the Brig Cyprus*, London: Rupert Hart-Davis.

Copeland, R., 1823, *An introduction to the practice of nautical surveying ... translated from the French of C.F. Beautemps-Beaupré*, London: R. H. Lawrie.

Cornell, C., 1974, *The journal of Post Captain Nicolas Baudin*, Adelaide: Libraries Board of South Australia.

Day, A. A., 1991, 'Geophysical measurements in Tasmania in 1792', *The Australian Geologist* 80: 6–8.

De Beer, G., 1960, *The sciences were never at war*, London: T. Nelson.

Degérando, J. M. (ed. Moore, F. C. T.), 1969, *The observation of savage peoples*, London: Routledge.

Dening, G., 1996, 'The history in things and places', in Bonyhady, T. and Griffiths, T. *Prehistory to politics*, Carlton: Melbourne University Press: 85–97.

Dixon, R.M.W., 1980, *The languages of Australia*, Cambridge: Cambridge University Press.

Dunbar, S., 1978, 'In reminiscence of Recherche', in Gee, H. and Fenton, J. *The Southwest book*, Hobart: Australian Conservation Foundation: 34.

Duyker, E., 2003, *Citizen Labillardière*, Carlton: Melbourne University Press.

——, 2006, 'In search of Jean Piron', *National Library of Australia News*, 16 March: 7–10.

Duyker, E. and M. (eds and trans), 2001, *Bruny d'Entrecasteaux voyage to Australia and the Pacific 1791–1793*, Carlton: Melbourne University Press.

——, 2004, 'A French garden in Tasmania: the legacy of Félix Delahaye (1767–1829)', *Explorations* 37: 3–43.

Dyer, C., 2005, *The French explorers and the Aboriginal Australians*, St Lucia: University of Queensland Press.

Estensen, M., 2005, *The life of George Bass*, Crows Nest: Allen & Unwin.

Evans, Kathryn, 1993, 'Shore-based whaling in Tasmania — Historical Research Project', 2 vols, Unpublished: Report for the Parks and Wildlife Service, Tasmania.

Flanagan, Richard, 2001, *Gould's book of fish: a novel in 12 fish*, Sydney: Pan Macmillan.

Flinders, M., 1814, *A voyage to Terra Australis*. 2 vols, London: G. and W. Nicol.

Greenhill, B., 1970, *James Cook, the opening of the Pacific*, London: National Maritime Museum.

Guicheteau, T. and Kernéis, J. -P., 1990, Medical aspects of the voyages of exploration, in Hardy, J. and Frost, A. (eds), *European voyaging towards Australia*, Canberra: 67-9.

Hiatt, B., 1969, 'Cremation in Aboriginal Australia', *Mankind* 7: 104–19.

Horner, F., 1987, *The French reconnaissance: Baudin in Australia 1801-1803*, Carlton: Melbourne University Press.

——, 1995, *Looking for La Pérouse*, Carlton: Melbourne University Press.

Hunt, S. and Carter, P., 1999, *Terre Napoléon: Australia through French eyes 1800–1804*, Sydney: Historic Houses Trust.

Ingleton, G. C., 1952, *True patriots all*, Sydney: Angus and Robertson.

Jones, Rhys, 1970, 'Tasmanian Aborigines and dogs', *Mankind* 7: 256–71.

——, 1974, 'Tasmanian tribes', in Tindale, N. B., *Aboriginal tribes of Australia*, Berkeley: University of California Press.

——, 1988, 'Images of natural man', in Bonnemains, J., Forsyth, E. and Smith, B. (eds), 1988, *Baudin in Australian waters*, Melbourne: Oxford University Press: 35–64.

Kostoglou, P., 1993, 'Historic timber-getting between Cockle Creek and Lune River', Unpublished: Archaeology of the Tasmanian Timber Industry No. 4, Forestry Commission, Tasmania.

Labillardière, M., 1800, *Voyage in search of La Pérouse*, London: John Stockdale.

Lempriere, T. J., 1954 [1939], *The penal settlements of early Van Diemen's Land*, [Launceston]: Royal Society of Tasmania.

Lilley, F. E. M., 1991, 'D'Entrecasteaux in Van Diemen's Land 1792; a bicentenary in geomagnetism', *Geophysics Down Under* (Geological Society of Australia) Newsletter of Specialist Group on Solid-Earth Geophysics, 14 December: 5–6.

Lilley, F. E. M. and Day, A. A., 1993, 'D'Entrecasteaux, 1792: celebrating a bicentennial in geomagnetism', *Eos, Transactions American Geophysical Union* 74: 97, 102–3.

Long, C. R., [1903], *Stories of Australian exploration*, Melbourne: Whitcombe and Tombs.

McBryde, I., 1997, The ambiguities of authenticity – rock of faith or shifting sands? *Conservation and Management of Archaeological Sites* 2: 93-100.

Mackaness, G. (ed.), 1947, *Some private correspondence of Sir John and Lady Jane Franklin*, Sydney: D.S. Ford.

Marquis-Kyle, P. and Walker, M., 2004, *The Illustrated Burra Charter*, Burwood: Australia ICOMOS.

Meehan, B., 1967, 'The food quest and the economy of the Tasmanian Aborigines', *Oceania* 38: 99–133, 190–219.

Mulvaney, D. J., 1958, 'The Australian Aborigines, 1606 – 1929: opinion and fieldwork', *Historical Studies* 8: 131–51, 297–315.

——, 1989, *Encounters in place: outsiders and Aboriginal Australians 1606 – 1985*, St Lucia: University of Queensland Press.

Mulvaney, D. J. and White, J. P. (eds), 1987, *Australians to 1788*, Sydney: Fairfax, Syme and Weldon.

Mulvaney, John, 2001 / 2002, 'Uranium and cultural heritage values', *Dissent* 7 (summer): 47–50.

Nash, M., 2003, *The bay whalers. Tasmania's shore-based whaling industry*, Hobart: Navarine Publishing.

Péron, F., 1809, *A voyage of discovery in the Southern Hemisphere*, London.

Pearson, M., 2005, *Great southern land. The maritime exploration of Terra Australis*, Canberra: Australian Government.

Plomley, N. J. B. (ed.), 1966, *Friendly mission: the Tasmanian journals and papers of George Augustus Robinson*, Hobart: Tasmanian Historical Research Association.

——, 1983, *The Baudin expedition and the Tasmanian Aborigines*, Hobart: Blubber Head Press.

Plomley, B. and Piard-Bernier, J., 1993, *The General*, Launceston: Queen Victoria Museum.

Potts, B. M. and Reid, J. B., 2003, 'Tasmania's eucalypts: their place in science', *Papers and Proceedings of the Royal Society of Tasmania* 137: 21–36.

Poulson, B., 2004, *Recherche Bay. A short history*, Southport: Southport Community Centre.

Pretyman, E. R., 1954, 'Pirates at Recherche Bay', *Papers and Proceedings of the Royal Society of Tasmania* 88: 119–28.

Rae-Ellis, V., 1988, *Black Robinson*, Carlton: Melbourne University Press.

Richard, H., 1986, *Le Voyage de d'Entrecasteaux a la recherché de La Pérouse*, Paris: Editions du Comité des Travaux Historiques et Scientifiques.

——, 1990, 'The d'Entrecasteaux expedition', in Hardy, J. and Frost, A. (eds), *European voyaging towards Australia*, Canberra: Australian Academy of the Humanities: 95–8.

Richards, B., 2000, 'James Craig a lot of vision, a little compromise', *Signals* 52 (September – November): 6–9.

Robson, L., 1983, *A history of Tasmania*, Melbourne: Oxford University Press.

Rossel, E. P. E. de, 1808, *Voyage de d'Entrecasteaux envoyé à la recherché de la Pérouse*, Paris: Imprimérie impériale.

Scheibinger, L. and Swan, C. (eds), 2005, *Colonial botany: science, commerce, politics in the early modern world*, Philadelphia: University of Philadelphia Press.

Sissons, D, 'The voyage of the *Cyprus* mutineers. Did they ever enter Japanese waters?', *Journal of Pacific History*, forthcoming.

Smith, B., 1960, *European vision and the South Pacific 1768 – 1850*, Oxford: Clarendon Press.

Taillemite, E., 1990, 'Shipboard life', in Hardy, J. and Frost, A. (eds), *European voyaging towards Australia*, Canberra: Australian Academy of the Humanities: 57–60.

Toghill, J., 1978, *The James Craig: her history, recovery and restoration*, Sydney: Reed.

Twelvetrees, W. H., 1902, *Report on the coalfield in the neighbourhood of Recherche Bay*, Launceston: Government Geologist.

Tylor, E. B., 1894, 'On the Tasmanians as representatives of Palaeolithic man', *Journal Anthropological Institute* 22: 141–52.

Tyndale-Biscoe, H., 2004, 'Recherche Bay: a site of great significance', *Australian Academy of Science Newsletter* No. 60: 3.

Watt, J., 1990, 'The health of sailors', in Hardy, J. and Frost, A. (eds), *European voyaging towards Australia*, Canberra: Australian Academy of the Humanities: 47–56.

West, J., 1852, *The history of Tasmania*, 2 vols, Launceston.

Whitham, L., 1983, The Catamaran Colliery and its transport systems. *Papers and Proceedings Tasmanian Historical Research Association* 30: 69-81.

Woolley, R. and Smith, W., 2004, *A history of the Huon and far south*, Huon Valley Council.

www.ingramcontent.com/pod-product-compliance
Lightning Source LLC
Chambersburg PA
CBHW060950170426
43201CB00032B/2421